JOURNEY INTO
GOD'S WORD

Also by J. Scott Duvall and J. Daniel Hays

*Dictionary of Biblical Prophecy
and End Times* (with C. Marvin Pate)

Grasping God's Word

Grasping God's Word Workbook

*Zondervan Get an A! Study Guides/
Grasping God's Word Laminated Sheet*

Preaching God's Word (with Terry G. Carter)

j. scott
DUVALL

j. daniel
HAYS

authors of
Grasping God's Word

JOURNEY INTO
GOD'S WORD

ZONDERVAN®

ZONDERVAN

Journey into God's Word
Copyright © 2008 by J. Scott Duvall and J. Daniel Hays

This title is also available as a Zondervan ebook.
Visit www.zondervan.com/ebooks.

Requests for information should be addressed to:
Zondervan, 3900 *Sparks Dr. SE, Grand Rapids, Michigan 49546*

Library of Congress Cataloging-in-Publication Data

Duvall, J. Scott.
    Journey into God's word : your guide to understanding and applying the Bible / J.
   Scott Duvall and J. Daniel Hays.
       p. cm.
    Includes bibliographical references.
    ISBN 978-0-310-27513-8
    1. Bible—Criticism, interpretation, etc. I. Hays, J. Daniel, 1953– II. Title.
   BS511.3.D88 2007
   220.601—dc22   2007026428

Interior design: Nancy Wilson

Printed in the United States of America

15 16 17 18 19 20 21 /DCI/ 34 33 32 31 30 29 28 27 26 25 24 23 22 21 20 19 18 17

*To those who labor to teach
God's people how to understand
and apply God's Word*

Contents

Preface

*S*ince *Grasping God's Word* appeared in 2001 (second edition in 2005), not many weeks go by without one of us getting an email asking about resources for adapting the material to a local church setting. Until now we have had to say, "We wish we had more to offer, but all we can suggest is that you hit the high points in our 462-page textbook." With the publication of *Journey into God's Word* we can now offer a resource that is custom-made for the local church (e.g., any group study with adults or older youth).

Journey into God's Word is an abridgment of *Grasping God's Word*, the textbook that has been used successfully in many college and seminary classrooms. We have captured the heart of *GGW* and reduced the length by omitting some of the examples and discussions that were more specialized, along with a few chapters. If you have enjoyed the original, we think you will like the abridgment since the approach is the same.

The opening chapter describes the process of reading and applying the Bible, a process we describe as an interpretive journey. Next, we talk about the skills and insights necessary for reading Scripture accurately and responsibly. Finally, we discuss how to read and apply specific sections of both the Old and New Testaments. Each chapter closes with discussion questions and hands-on assignments that allow you to apply what you have learned. Also, you might consider the following eight-week teaching schedule for local churches:

Week 1: Chapters 1 (Interpretive Journey) and 7 (Bible Translations)
Week 2: Chapters 2 and 3 (Reading Carefully)
Week 3: Chapters 5 (Historical-Cultural Context) and 6 (Literary Context)

Our prayer is that *Journey into God's Word* will be your faithful guide in one of the most satisfying adventures of your life — exploring the depths of God's Word. May your relationship with God grow deeper and stronger as you learn how to hear and do what he has communicated to us.

J. Scott Duvall
J. Daniel Hays

Summer 2007

The Interpretive Journey

A wrinkled old man in the mountains of Ethiopia sips coffee and peers through weathered, ancient reading glasses at his worn Amharic Bible to read once again the story of David and Goliath. A middle-aged woman is bouncing along on a bus in Buenos Aires, reading and reflecting on Psalm 1. A young Korean executive, on his way home to Seoul from a business trip to Singapore, flies above the clouds at 35,000 feet, reading and pondering the words of the apostle Paul in Romans 5. And in a dorm room in San Diego, California, a young college student polishes off another Mountain Dew and then looks back down at her laptop computer to finish reading Mark's account of how Jesus miraculously calmed a raging storm on the Sea of Galilee.

People all over the world love reading the Bible — and they have loved it for thousands of years. Why? People read the Bible because it is a fascinating book, filled with gripping stories and challenging exhortations. People read it because it is an important book, dealing with the big issues of life — God, eternal life, death, love, sin, and morals. People read it because they believe that in the Bible God speaks to them through written words. The Bible encourages us, lifts our spirits, comforts us, guides us, chides us, builds us up, gives us hope, and brings us close to the living God.

Some parts of the Bible are easy to understand, but much of it is not. Most Christians, however, desire to understand all of God's Word, not just the easy portions. Many of us want to be able to dig deeper into that Word. We want to see more and to understand more of the biblical text.

We also want to know that we understand the Bible correctly. That is, we want to be confident that we can pull the actual truth out of a text and not just develop an arbitrary, fanciful, or incorrect interpretation. This book is designed for such people.

The process of interpreting and grasping the Bible is similar to embarking on a *journey*. Reading the text thoroughly and carefully lies at the beginning of the journey. From this careful reading we become able to determine what the passage meant in the biblical context—that is, what it meant to the biblical audience.

Often, however, when we try to apply this meaning directly to ourselves, we run into problems. We are separated from the biblical audience by culture and customs, language, situation, and a vast expanse of time. These differences form a barrier—a *river* that separates us from the text and that often prohibits us from grasping the meaning of the text for ourselves.

If that were not enough, the Old Testament widens the river by adding another major interpretive barrier that separates us from the audience. Between the Old Testament biblical audience and Christian readers today lies a change in *covenant*. We as New Testament believers are under the new covenant, and we approach God through the sacrifice of Christ. The Old Testament people, however, were under the old covenant, and for them the law was central. In other words, the theological situation for the two groups is different. There is a covenant barrier between the Old Testament audience and us because we are under different covenants.

Thus, the river between the Old Testament text and us consists not only of culture, language, situation, and time, but also of covenant. We have much more in common with the New Testament audience; yet even in the New Testament, the different culture, language, and specific situations can present a formidable barrier to our understanding of the meaning of the text. The river is often too deep and too wide simply to wade across.

As a result, today's Christian is often uncertain about how to interpret much of the Bible. How should we understand Leviticus 19:19, which prohibits wearing a garment made of two types of material? Does this mean that obedient Christians should wear only 100 percent cotton clothes? In

Judges 6:37 Gideon puts out a fleece in order to confirm what God had told him. Does this mean that *we* should put out fleeces when we seek God's leading?

Passages in the New Testament are not always much clearer. For example, Peter walks on the water in Matthew 14:29. Does this mean that *we* should attempt to walk on water in our obedience to Christ? If not, what does it mean and how can we apply that passage to our lives? Even if we cannot walk on water, how do we cross the river that separates us from the text?

Any attempt to interpret and to apply the Bible involves trying to cross the river. While often unconscious of their interpretive method, many Christians today nonetheless frequently employ an *intuitive* or *feels-right approach* to interpretation. If the text looks as if it could be applied directly, then they attempt to apply it directly. If not, then they take a *spiritualizing approach* to the meaning—an approach that borders on allegorizing the biblical text (which shows little or no sensitivity to the biblical context). Or else they simply shrug their shoulders and move onto another passage, ignoring the meaning of the text altogether.

Such approaches will never land us safely on the other side of the river. Those using the intuitive approach blindly wade out into the river, hoping that the water is not more than knee deep. Sometimes they are fortunate and stumble onto a sandbar, but often they step out into deep water, and they end up washed ashore somewhere downstream. Those who spiritualize, by contrast, try to jump the river in one grand leap, but they also end up washed ashore downstream with their intuitive buddies. Shrugging or ignoring a passage is to remain on the far side of the river and simply to gaze across without even attempting to cross.

Many Christians are admittedly uncomfortable with such approaches, recognizing the somewhat willy-nilly methodology and the extreme subjectivity involved, but they continue to use them because they are the only method they know. How do we move from the world of the biblical audience to the world of today?

This book addresses how to cross over that river into the world of today. We need a valid, legitimate approach to the Bible, one that is not based strictly on intuition and feeling. We need an approach that derives meaning from within the text, but one that also crosses over to the situation for today's Christian.

We also need a consistent approach, one that can be used on any passage. Such an approach should eliminate the habit of skipping over texts and surfing along through the Bible looking for passages that might apply. A consistent approach should allow us to dig into any passage with a method to determine the meaning of that text for us today. We need an approach that does not leave us stranded on the banks of the interpretive river and one that does not dump us into the river to be washed ashore downstream. We need a way to study the Bible to cross over the river with validity and accuracy. Our goal in this book is to take you on the journey across the river, to transport you from the text and the world of the biblical audience to a valid understanding and application of the text for Christians today.

Basics of the Journey

Keep in mind that our goal is to grasp the meaning of the text God has intended. We do not create meaning out of a text; rather, we seek to find the meaning that is already there. However, we recognize that we cannot apply the meaning for the ancient audience directly to us today because of the river that separates us (culture, time, situation, covenant, etc.). Following the steps of the Interpretive Journey provides us with a procedure that allows us to take the meaning for the ancient audience and to cross over the river to determine a legitimate meaning for us today.

This journey works on the premise that the Bible is a record of God's communication of himself and his will to us. We revere the Bible and treat it as holy because it is the Word of God and because God reveals himself to us through this Word. Many texts in the Bible are specific, concrete, revelatory expressions of broader, universal realities or theological principles. While the specifics of a particular passage may only apply to the particular situation of the biblical audience, the theological principles revealed in that text are applicable to all of God's people at all times. The theological principle, therefore, has meaning and application both to the ancient biblical audience and to Christians today.

Because the theological principle has meaning and application to both audiences, it functions as a bridge spanning the river of differences. Rather than blindly wading out into the river, foolishly attempting to jump across the river in one short hop, or wishfully gazing at the other shore without ever crossing, we can safely cross over the river on the bridge that the theological principle provides. Constructing this *principlizing bridge* will be one of the critical steps in our Interpretive Journey.

Thus, our journey starts with a careful reading of the text. Our final destination is to grasp the meaning of the text so that it changes our lives. It is an exciting trip, but one that requires hard work. There are no easy shortcuts.

The basic Interpretive Journey involves four steps:

Step 1: Grasping the Text in Their Town.

What did the text mean to the biblical audience?

The first part of Step 1 is to read the text carefully and observe the details. In Step 1, try to see as much as possible in the text. Look, look, and look again, observing all that you can. Scrutinize the grammar and analyze all significant words. Likewise, study the historical and literary contexts. How does your passage relate to the one that precedes it and the one that follows?

After completing all of this study, synthesize the meaning of the passage for the biblical audience into one or two sentences. That is, write out what the passage meant for the biblical audience. Use past-tense verbs and refer to the biblical audience. For example:

God commanded the Israelites in Joshua 1 to ...

Jesus encouraged his disciples by ...

Paul exhorted the Ephesians to ...

Be specific. Do not generalize or try to develop theological principles yet.

Step 2: Measuring the Width of the River to Cross.

What are the differences between the biblical audience and us?

As mentioned above, the Christian today is separated from the biblical audience by differences in culture, language, situation, time, and often

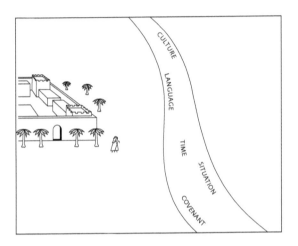

covenant. These differences form a river that hinders us from moving straight from meaning in their context to meaning in ours. The width of the river, however, varies from passage to passage. Sometimes it is extremely wide, requiring a long, substantial bridge for crossing. Other times, however, it is a narrow creek that we can easily hop over. It is obviously important to know just how wide the river is before we start trying to construct a principlizing bridge across it.

In Step 2 you will take a good hard look at the river and determine just how wide it is for the passage you are studying. In this step you look for significant *differences* between our situation today and the situation of the biblical audience. If you are studying an Old Testament passage, also be sure to identify those significant theological differences that came as a result of the life and work of Jesus Christ.

In addition, whether in the Old Testament or in the New Testament, try to identify any unique aspects of the *situation* of your passage. For example, in Joshua 1:1–9, the people of Israel are preparing to enter the Promised Land. Moses has just died and Joshua has been appointed to take his place. In this passage God speaks to Joshua to encourage him to be strong and faithful in the upcoming conquest of the land. What are the differences? We are not entering or conquering the Promised Land.

We are not the new leaders of the nation of Israel. We are not under the old covenant.

Step 3: Crossing the Principlizing Bridge.

What is the theological principle in this text?

This is perhaps the most challenging step. In it you are looking for the theological principle or principles that are reflected in the meaning of the text you identified in Step 1. Remember that this theological principle is part of the *meaning*. Your task is not to create the meaning but to discover the meaning intended by the author. As God gives specific expressions to specific biblical audiences, he is also giving universal theological teachings for all of his people through these same texts.

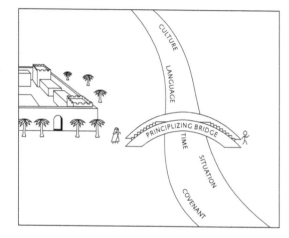

To determine the theological principle, first recall the differences you identified in Step 2. Next, try to identify any *similarities* between the situation of the biblical audience and our situation. For example, consider Joshua 1:1–9 again. Recall, of course, the differences that we identified in Step 2. But then note the similarities between the biblical situation and our own: We are also the people of God, in covenant relationship (new covenant); while we are not the leaders of Israel, nonetheless many of us are in leadership positions in the church; we are not invading the Promised Land, but we are seeking to obey the will of God and to accomplish what he has commanded us to do.

After reviewing the differences and identifying the similarities, return to the meaning for the biblical audience that you described in Step 1 and try to identify a broader theological principle reflected in the text, but also one that relates to the similarities between us and the biblical audience. We will use this theological principle as the *principlizing bridge* by which we can cross over the river of barriers.

In addition, during this step you must enter into the *parts-whole spiral*. That is, you reflect back and forth between the text and the teachings of the rest of Scripture. The theological principle that you derive should not only be present in the passage, but it must also be congruent with the rest of Scripture. We can summarize the criteria for formulating the theological principle with the following:

- The principle should be reflected in the text.
- The principle should be timeless and not tied to a specific situation.
- The principle should not be bound to one particular culture.
- The principle should correspond to the teaching of the rest of Scripture.
- The principle should be relevant to both the biblical audience and the contemporary audience.

Write out the theological principle (or principles) in one or two sentences. Use present-tense verbs.

Step 4: Grasping the Text in Our Town.

How should individual Christians today apply the theological principle in their lives?

In Step 4 we apply the theological principle to the specific situation of individual Christians in the church today. We cannot leave the meaning of the text stranded in an abstract theological principle. We must now grapple with how we should respond to that principle in our town. How does it apply in real-life situations today?

While for each passage there will usually only be a few (and often only one) theological principles relevant for all Christians today, there will be numerous possibilities for application. This is because Christians today find themselves in many different specific situations. Each of us will grasp and apply the same theological principle in slightly different ways, depending on our current life situation and where we are in our

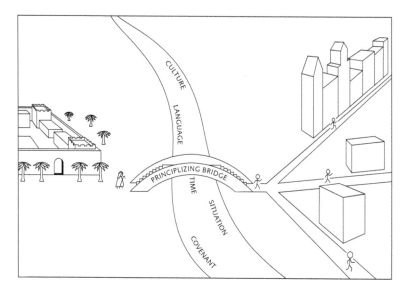

relationship with God. In our illustration, we have tried to show the different applications possible by showing different individuals traveling on different streets. (The application step will be discussed in much more detail in chapter 8.)

So, the Interpretive Journey as a whole looks like this:

Step 1: Grasp the text in their town.
Step 2: Measure the width of the river to cross.
Step 3: Cross the principlizing bridge.
Step 4: Grasp the text in our town.

An Example — Joshua 1:1 – 9

We have mentioned Joshua 1:1 – 9 several times already. Let's make the formal trip from this Old Testament passage to life today in order to illustrate how the Interpretive Journey works.

The passage is as follows:

> [1]After the death of Moses the servant of the LORD, the LORD said to Joshua son of Nun, Moses' aide: [2]"Moses my servant is dead. Now then, you and all these people, get ready to cross the Jordan River into

the land I am about to give to them—to the Israelites. ³I will give you every place where you set your foot, as I promised Moses. ⁴Your territory will extend from the desert and to Lebanon and from the great river, the Euphrates—all the Hittite country—to the Great Sea on the west. ⁵No one will be able to stand up against you all the days of your life. As I was with Moses, so I will be with you; I will never leave you nor forsake you.

⁶"Be strong and courageous, because you will lead these people to inherit the land I swore to their forefathers to give them. ⁷Be strong and very courageous. Be careful to obey all the law my servant Moses gave you; do not turn from it to the right or to the left, that you may be successful wherever you go. ⁸Do not let this Book of the Law depart from your mouth; meditate on it day and night, so that you may be careful to do everything written in it. Then you will be prosperous and successful. ⁹Have I not commanded you? Be strong and courageous. Do not be terrified; do not be discouraged, for the Lord your God will be with you wherever you go."

Step 1: What did the text mean to the biblical audience?

The Lord commanded Joshua, the new leader of Israel, to draw strength and courage from God's empowering presence, to be obedient to the law of Moses, and to meditate on the law so that he would be successful in the conquest of the Promised Land.

Step 2: What are the differences between the biblical audience and us?

We are not leaders of the nation Israel (although some of us may be leaders in the church). We are not embarking on the conquest of Canaan, the Promised Land. We are not under the old covenant of law.

Step 3: What is the theological principle in this text?

To be effective in serving God and successful in the task to which he has called us, we must draw strength and courage from his presence. We must also be obedient to God's Word, meditating on it constantly.

Step 4: How should individual Christians today apply the theological principle in their lives?

There are numerous possible applications. Here are a few suggested ones:

- Spend more time meditating on God's Word by listening to Christian music as you ride in your car.

- If God calls you to a new, scary ministry, such as teaching fourth-grade Sunday school, then be strengthened and encouraged by his empowering presence. Be obedient, keeping a focus on the Scriptures.
- If you are in a church leadership position, realize that successful Christian leadership requires strength and courage that flows from the presence of God.

Journey into God's Word

The Interpretive Journey is actually a blueprint for this book. In chapters 2 and 3 we learn how to observe and read carefully. We start with smaller, simpler units of text and then move on to more complex and longer units of text. In chapters 4, 5, and 6 we spend time discussing contexts, both the context of the contemporary reader as well as the cultural-historical and literary contexts of the ancient text. In chapter 7 we will learn more about Bible translations. All of these chapters give us skills necessary to move through Steps 1 and 2 of the Journey. Chapter 8 talks about meaning and application, both important topics for navigating Steps 3 and 4 of the Journey.

Next we move into the actual practice of interpreting and applying the New Testament. We teach you how to journey through different types of New Testament literature. Chapters 9 – 12 cover, respectively, New Testament letters, the Gospels, Acts, and the book of Revelation. These chapters pull together everything you learned earlier and show you how to apply your new skills to the New Testament.

Finally, we look at some of the specific challenges and opportunities of interpreting and applying passages from the different Old Testament genres. Chapters 13 – 15 sharpen your tools for understanding and applying passages from a range of Old Testament literature: Law, Prophets, and Psalms.

Are you ready to move forward into the exciting realm of interpretation and application? There are lots of interesting biblical passages ahead of you. Work hard! The rewards are great.

Discussion Questions

1. What is wrong with the "intuitive" method of interpretation?
2. What are the four steps of the Interpretive Journey?
3. What are the differences that determine the width of the river to cross?
4. What are the guidelines for developing theological principles?

Serious Reading

2

Serious Reading and Love Letters

What is serious reading? Consider the following episode about a "serious" reader:

How to Read a Love Letter

This young man has just received his first love letter. He may read it three or four times, but he is just beginning. To read it as accurately as he would like would require several dictionaries and a good deal of close work with a few experts of etymology and philology.

However, he will do all right without them.

He will ponder over the exact shade of meaning of every word, every comma. She has headed the letter "Dear John." What, he asks himself, is the exact significance of those words? Did she refrain from saying "Dearest" because she was bashful? Would "My Dear" have sounded too formal?

Maybe she would have said "Dear So-and-so" to anybody! A worried frown will now appear on his face. But it disappears as soon as he really gets to thinking about the first sentence. She certainly wouldn't have written that to anybody!

And so he works his way through the letter, one moment perched blissfully on a cloud, the next moment huddled miserably behind an eight ball. It has started a hundred questions in his mind. He could quote it by heart. In fact, he will—to himself—for weeks to come.[1]

This lovesick boy is a good reader because he scrutinizes the text for all the details, even the most minute. One of the most critical skills needed in reading the Bible is the ability to *see* the details. Most of us read the Bible too quickly and we skip over the details of the text. However, the meaning of the Bible is intertwined into the details of every sentence. Our first step in understanding a biblical text is to observe as many details as possible. At this early stage of analysis, try to refrain from *interpreting* or *applying* the text. These steps are important, but they come later, after the *observing* step. Our first step is to read *seriously*, to note as many details as possible, to *observe* our text as closely as Crime Scene Investigators do a crime scene.

Keep in mind that we are not yet asking the question, "What does the text mean?" We are simply asking, "What does the text say?" We have not yet begun to explore the implications of our observations. Also, do not limit your observations to so-called *deep insights* or highly important features. At the observation step we want to see everything, all the details. Later in the book we will tackle the problem of sorting through the details to determine meaning.

Work hard! Dig deep! The feast awaits you!

Things to Look for in Sentences

1. Repetition of words

Look for words that repeat. Be sure to note any words that repeat within the sentence you are studying. Then survey the sentences around the text you are reading and look for repetition in the larger passage.

For example, read 1 John 2:15–17:

> [15]Do not love the world or anything in the world. If anyone loves the world, the love of the Father is not in him. [16]For everything in the world — the cravings of sinful man, the lust of his eyes and the boasting of what he has and does — comes not from the Father but from the world. [17]The world and its desires pass away, but the man who does the will of God lives forever.

Which word repeats in the first sentence? Does this word (*world*) appear in the next sentence as well? How many times in this passage does *world* occur? Is it in every sentence? Does it always have the definite article *the*, as in *the world*? Did you also notice the repetition of *love*? How many times does *love* occur? Simply by observing the repetition of words, we have an early indication of what the passage may be about. It has something to do with the world—in particular, about loving the world.

Let's look at word repetition in a few other passages as well. Look up the following texts and note the number of times the words listed are repeated:

John 15:1–10 (look for *remain*)

Matthew 6:1–18 (look for *father*)

1 Corinthians 15:50–54 (look for *perishable* and *imperishable*)

2. Contrasts

Look for items, ideas, or individuals that are contrasted with each other. For an example of contrast, take a look at Proverbs 14:31:

> He who oppresses the poor shows contempt for their Maker,
>   but whoever is kind to the needy honors God.

This passage contrasts two different types of people. They are contrasted in the way they treat the poor and in the way that this behavior toward the poor reflects their attitude toward God. One type oppresses the poor, and this action reflects contempt for God since he is their Creator. The other type of person is kind to the poor; his action toward the poor honors God.

What is being contrasted in Proverbs 15:1?

> A gentle answer turns away wrath,
>   but a harsh word stirs up anger.

The New Testament writers frequently use contrasts as well. Read Romans 6:23 and identify the two contrasts:

> For the wages of sin is death, but the gift of God is eternal life in Christ Jesus our Lord.

3. Comparison

Contrast focuses on differences, whereas comparison focuses on similarities. Look for items, ideas, or individuals that are compared with each other. Proverbs 25:26 provides a good Old Testament example:

Like a muddied spring or a polluted well
 is a righteous man who gives way to the wicked.

How is a righteous man who gives way to the wicked like a muddied spring? Because the spring, like the man, was once clean, pure, and useful, but now is contaminated and useless for service.

A wonderful comparison is made in Isaiah 40:31, where the renewal of strength received from placing one's hope in the Lord is compared to the soaring of eagles.

… but those who hope in the LORD
 will renew their strength.
They will soar on wings like eagles;
 they will run and not grow weary,
 they will walk and not be faint.

Good Bible study can make you soar like an eagle, too. So read on.

4. Lists

Any time you encounter a list of more than two items, identify it as a list. Write the list down and explore the significance of the list. Is there any order to the list? Are the items in the list grouped in any way? For example, what three things are listed in 1 John 2:16?

For everything in the world—the craving of sinful man, the lust of his eyes and the boasting of what he has and does—comes not from the Father but from the world.

What is listed in Galatians 5:22–23?

But the fruit of the Spirit is love, joy, peace, patience, kindness, goodness, faithfulness, gentleness, and self-control.

What is listed in Galatians 5:19–20?

The acts of the sinful nature are obvious: sexual immorality, impurity and debauchery; idolatry and witchcraft; hatred, discord, jealousy, fits of rage, selfish ambition, dissensions, factions and envy; drunkenness, orgies, and the like.

5. Cause and Effect

Often the biblical writers will state a *cause* and then the *effect* of that cause. The *effect* is a result or a consequence of the *cause*.

Earlier we looked at Proverbs 15:1 and found that the verse contained a contrast. It also has two cause-and-effect relationships. Take look at it again:

> A gentle answer turns away wrath,
> but a harsh word stirs up anger.

The first cause is *a gentle answer.* What is the effect of this cause? It turns away wrath. The second cause is *a harsh word.* And what does it result in? As we all well know, it stirs up anger.

Let's also look at Romans 6:23 again:

> For the wages of sin is death, but the gift of God is eternal life in Christ Jesus our Lord.

In this passage *sin* is the cause and *death* the effect.

Likewise, read Romans 12:2:

> Do not conform any longer to the pattern of this world, but be transformed by the renewing of your mind. Then you will be able to test and approve what God's will is — his good, pleasing and perfect will.

What is the cause? Our transformation through the renewing of our minds. What is the associated effect? The effect is the ability to discern God's will.

As you can see, cause-and-effect relationships play an important role in the Bible. Always be on the lookout for them.

6. Figures of Speech

Figures of speech are images in which words are used in a sense other than the normal, literal sense. For example, think about the lamp image in Psalm 119:105:

> Your word is a lamp to my feet
> and a light for my path.

God's Word is not a literal *lamp* to light up the trail for us. Rather, it is a figurative *lamp* that allows us to see our way through life (*feet/path*) clearly. Note that both *lamp* and *feet/path* are figures of speech.

As you observe biblical texts, always note and identify any figures of speech that occur. Try to visualize the figure of speech. Ask: "What image is the author trying to convey with the figure of speech?" For example, consider Isaiah 40:31 again:

> ...but those who hope in the LORD
>   will renew their strength
> They will soar on wings like eagles;
>   they will run and not grow weary,
>   they will walk and not be faint.

Soaring on wings like eagles is a figure of speech. Can you visualize the image—soaring up high ... coasting on a warm air current ... gliding along without even flapping your wings?

Figures of speech are powerful literary forms because they paint images that we can relate to emotionally.

7. Conjunctions

If we imagine the biblical text to be like a brick house, then conjunctions are the mortar that holds the bricks (phrases and sentences) together. One critical aspect of careful reading is to note all of the conjunctions (*and, for, but, therefore, since, because,* etc.). Our tendency is to skip right over them! But don't do it. Without the mortar the bricks would fall into a jumbled mess. So always take note of the conjunctions and then identify their purpose or function. That is, try to determine what it is that the conjunction connects.

For example, if you encounter the conjunction *but,* you might suspect some sort of contrast. Look in the text for the things being contrasted by this conjunction. Recall Romans 6:23:

> For the wages of sin is death, *but* the gift of God is eternal life in Christ Jesus our Lord.

The conjunction *but* indicates a contrast between the wages of sin (death) and the gift of God (eternal life).

Therefore or *so* usually presents some type of conclusion based on earlier arguments or reasons. When you encounter a *therefore*, read back into the text and determine what the earlier reason was. Sometimes the reason is easy to find, lying out in the open in the previous verse. However, at other times, the earlier reason is more difficult to find. It may refer to the larger message of several previous chapters.

8. Verbs—Where All the Action Is

Verbs are important because they communicate the action of the sentence. As you observe the text, be sure to note the verbal action. Try to identify what kind of verb is used. Is the verb a past, present, or future tense verb (*I went, I go, I will go*)? Does it present a progressive idea; that is, does it have continued action (*I was going, I am going, I will be going*)? Is it an imperative verb? Imperatives are verbs that command someone to do something (*Go!*). Be especially sure to note all imperative verbs! These are often God's commands to us.

Note the list of imperative verbs in Ephesians 4:2–3:

> Be completely humble and gentle; be patient, bearing with one another in love. Make every effort to keep the unity of the Spirit through the bond of peace.

Another important distinction to look for in verbs is whether they are active or passive. Active verbs are those where the subject is doing the action (Bill *hit* the ball). Passive verbs are those verbs where the subject is acted upon (Bill *was hit* by the ball). This distinction is particularly important in Paul's letters because verbs often distinguish between what we do and what God has done for us.

Note the following active and passive verbs:

> Since, then, you *have been raised* (passive!) with Christ, *set* (active!) your hearts on things above, where Christ is seated (passive!) at the right hand of God. (Col. 3:1)

> In him we *were* also *chosen* (passive!), *having been predestined* (passive!) according to the plan of him who *works out* (active!) everything in conformity with the purpose of his will. (Eph. 1:11)

9. Pronouns

Pronouns are words that refer to other nouns (people, places, items, ideas) in the context. Pronouns include words such as *he, she, you, me, my, we, our,* and *it.* Note all pronouns and be sure to identify the antecedent (to whom or to what the pronoun refers).

Who is the *our* and *us* in Ephesians 1:3?

Praise be to the God and Father of *our* Lord Jesus Christ, who has blessed *us* in the heavenly realms with every spiritual blessing in Christ.

Identify all of the pronouns in the following text:

²⁷Whatever happens, conduct yourselves in a manner worthy of the gospel of Christ. Then, whether I come and see you or only hear about you in my absence, I will know that you stand firm in one spirit, contending as one man for the faith of the gospel ²⁸without being frightened in any way by those who oppose you. This is a sign to them that they will be destroyed, but that you will be saved — and that by God. ²⁹For it has been granted to you on behalf of Christ not only to believe on him, but also to suffer for him, ³⁰since you are going through the same struggle you saw I had, and now hear that I still have. (Philippians 1:27 – 30)

Discussion Questions

1. Read 1 John 1:5 – 7. Which "things to look for" from this chapter do you see in verse 5? In verse 6? In verse 7?
2. Read Romans 12:1 – 2. Which "things to look for" from this chapter do you see in verse 1? In verse 2?

Writing Assignment

Photocopy this page from 1 Timothy 6:17 – 19 and make as many observations as you can on this passage below.

[17]Command those who are rich in this present world not to be arro-

gant nor to put their hope in wealth, which is so uncertain, but to put

their hope in God, who richly provides us with everything for our enjoy-

ment. [18]Command them to do good, to be rich in good deeds, and to be

generous and willing to share. [19]In this way they will lay up treasure for

themselves as a firm foundation for the coming age, so that they may take

hold of the life that is truly life.

Keep Your Eye on the Horizon   3

In contrast to the last chapter, sometimes we need to turn our attention to the horizon. Sometimes we need to take a step back and notice the big picture around the passage we are studying. In chapter 2 you learned how to make observations at the sentence level. In this chapter you will continue to develop your skill in making observations, but we will shift the focus of your observation from sentences to paragraphs and even chapters and episodes. Keep looking! Keep observing! Keep digging into the Word of God!

1. General and Specific

Sometimes an author will introduce an idea with a general statement — that is, an overview or summary of their main idea. The author will then follow this general statement with the specifics of the idea. Often these specifics provide the supporting details that make the general idea true or explain it more completely. For example, I can make a *general* statement, "I like dessert." I can then explain this more fully with the *specific* details, "I like apple pie, strawberry shortcake, chocolate ice cream, and cheesecake." This is a movement from *general* to *specific*.

Although the biblical writers do not write of chocolate ice cream, they do often use the *general-to-specific* literary feature to communicate to us. For example, Paul makes a *general* statement in Galatians 5:16:

> So I say, live by the Spirit, and you will not gratify the desires of the sinful nature.

Living by the Spirit and gratifying the desires of the sinful nature are general statements. As readers we want to know more details or specifics about each of these. Paul obliges us and presents the specifics of gratifying "the desires of the sinful nature" in 5:19–21a:

> The acts of the sinful nature are obvious: sexual immorality, impurity and debauchery; idolatry and witchcraft; hatred, discord, jealousy, fits of rage, selfish ambition, dissensions, factions and envy; drunkenness, orgies, and the like....

Paul next presents the *specifics* of how to "live by the Spirit" in 5:22:

> But the fruit of the Spirit is love, joy, peace, patience, kindness, goodness, faithfulness, gentleness and self-control.

So Paul has presented a *general* statement in Galatians 5:16 and then moved to the associated *specific* statements in 5:19–22.

Also keep in mind that the authors will frequently reverse the order and go from *specific* to *general*. The writer will first list out the *specifics* ("I like apple pie, strawberry shortcake, chocolate ice cream, and cheesecake") and then recap the idea with a *general* statement summarizing the main point ("I like dessert").

2. Questions and Answers

Occasionally an author will raise a rhetorical question and then answer his own question. Paul does this several times in Romans. For instance, in Romans 6:1 he asks:

> What shall we say then? Shall we go on sinning so that grace may increase?

Paul then answers his own question in verse 2:

> By no means! We died to sin; how can we live in it any longer?

In the verses that follow, the apostle continues to discuss the answer to his opening question in Romans 6:1. Paul uses this type of question-and-answer format in numerous other places in Romans as well (3:1, 5, 9, 27–31; 4:1, 9; 6:15; 7:1, 7, 13; 8:31–35; 11:1, 7, 11).

This technique is not limited to Paul's letters. Mark uses the question-and-answer format in several places as the backdrop for the story of Jesus. For example, in Mark 2:1 – 3:6 there are five episodes that revolve around a question and an answer.

3. Dialogue

Dialogue, of course, overlaps slightly with the question-and-answer feature discussed above. The four questions in Mark 2:15 – 3:6 are part of an ongoing dialogue between Jesus and the Pharisees. Dialogue may seem at first glance to be too obvious to worry about. Clearly, in narrative material dialogue is employed frequently and is easy to spot. But do not simply read past the point of the dialogue. Note the fact that a dialogue is taking place. Then ask questions of the dialogue. Who are the participants? Who is speaking to whom? What is the setting? Are other people around? Are they listening? Are they participating in the dialogue? Is the dialogue an argument? A discussion? A lecture? Friendly chitchat? What is the point of the dialogue?

The stories of the Bible contain a multitude of wonderful dialogues. Recall Jesus' conversation with the Samaritan woman at the well in John 4. Another famous dialogue occurs between Peter and Jesus in John 13:6 – 10, where they discuss whether or not Jesus will wash Peter's feet. Clearly one of the most unusual discussions in the Bible is the conversation between Balaam and his donkey in Numbers 22.

4. Purpose and Result Statements

Always identify *purpose* and *result statements*. These are phrases or sentences that describe the reason, the result, or the consequence of some action. They are frequently introduced by result-oriented conjunctions such as *that, in order that, so that,* etc., but they can also be introduced with the simple infinitive (*to* plus a verb). The following examples illustrate the use of purpose statements:

> For we are God's workmanship, created in Christ Jesus *to* do good works. (Eph. 2:10)

> For God so loved the world *that* he gave his one and only Son. (John 3:16)

> You did not choose me, but I chose you and appointed you *to* go and bear fruit—fruit that will last. (John 15:16)

5. Means

When an action, a result, or a purpose is stated, look for the *means* that will bring about that action, result, or purpose. How is the action or result brought into reality? How is the purpose accomplished? For example, read the second half of Romans 8:13:

> ... but if *by the Spirit* you put to death the misdeeds of the body, you will live.

The *means* by which the misdeeds of the body are put to death is the Spirit.

Likewise, ponder a moment on Psalm 119:9:

> How can a young man keep his way pure?
> > By living according to your word.

The purpose or action desired is for a young man to keep his way pure. What is the *means*? By living according to God's Word.

6. Conditional Clauses

Identify all conditional clauses. These are clauses that present the conditions whereby some action, consequence, reality, or result will happen. The conditional aspect will usually be introduced by the conditional conjunction *if*; the result or consequence will occasionally be introduced by *then*, though often the result or consequence has no specific introductory words. Any time you encounter a conditional clause, always determine exactly what the required conditional action is (the *if* part) and what the result or consequence is (the *then* part).

Identify the conditional clause and the result or consequence in each of the following:

> If we claim to have fellowship with him yet walk in the darkness, we lie and do not live by the truth. (1 John 1:6)

Condition: if we claim to have fellowship with him yet walk in darkness
Result or consequence: we lie and do not live by the truth

> Therefore, if anyone is in Christ, he is a new creation; the old has gone, the new has come! (2 Cor. 5:17)

Condition: if anyone is in Christ
Result or consequence: he is a new creation; the old has gone, the new
has come

7. The Actions/Roles of People and the Actions/Roles of God

Biblical passages will often refer to actions that people do as well as actions that God does. Identify these and mark them separately. Ask the question, "What does God (the Father, the Son, or the Spirit) do in this passage?" and also, "What do people do in this passage?" Then ask whether or not there is any kind of connection between what God does and what people do.

For example, read Ephesians 5:1–2:

> Be imitators of God, therefore, as dearly loved children and live a life of love, just as Christ loved us and gave himself up for us as a fragrant offering and sacrifice to God.

What are the actions or roles of people in this passage? We are told to be imitators of God in the same way that children are imitators. We are also told to live a life of love as Christ did. What is Christ's or God's role in this passage? Christ's role was to offer himself up to God for us. God's role is to be the one who is imitated.

In addition, be sure to observe when references to God are made with relational terms (father, husband, king). For example, in Matthew 5:43–6:34 there are *eleven* references to God as "Father" (5:45, 48; 6:1, 4, 6, 8, 9, 14, 15, 18, 32). By his repeated use of" "Father" in this passage (from the Sermon on the Mount) Jesus is clearly trying to convey an idea of relationship to God as a Father (both his and ours).

8. Emotional Terms

The Bible is not a book of abstract, technical information. It is a book about relationships, primarily relationships between God and people. Emotions play a big role in relationships. This is frequently overlooked in biblical interpretation. As part of your careful reading, when you observe the text be sure to underscore words and phrases that have emotional overtones, that is, words that convey feeling and emotion. Also be sure to note terms such as "father, mother, child, daughter, son," and so on. These usually have underlying emotional connotations as well.

Read the following passage and note the emotional connotations of the italicized phrases and words:

> I *plead* with you, brothers, become like me, for I became like you. You have done me no wrong. As you know, it was because of an illness that I first preached the gospel to you. Even though my illness was a trial to you, you did not treat me with *contempt* or *scorn*. Instead, you *welcomed* me as if I were an angel of God, as if I were Christ Jesus himself. What has happened to all your *joy*? I can testify that, if you could have done so, you would have *torn out your eyes* and given them to me. Have I now become your *enemy* by telling you the truth? (Gal. 4:12 – 16)

Plead is much more emotional than *ask*, isn't it? Paul seems to have intentionally chosen strong emotional terms to express himself in this passage (and throughout Galatians). What feelings does Paul express here? Why does he bring up their past relationship, recalling how they once welcomed him? How strong is the phrase *torn out your eyes*? Likewise, what kind of connotations does the word *enemy* carry?

9. Connections between Paragraphs and Episodes

After reading carefully and observing thoroughly at the sentence level and at the paragraph level, it is important to ask how your paragraph (in the letters) or your episode (in the narratives) relates to the other paragraphs/ episodes that come before and after the one you are studying. What is the connection between your paragraph and the paragraph that precedes it? What about the paragraph that follows? How do they all relate?

So far we have focused on the relationship between phrases, clauses, and sentences. We looked at cause-and-effect relationships, general-to-specific relationships, conditional clauses with resultant or consequential effects, and other relational features within sentences and between sentences. These same features will also often connect paragraphs (in the letters) and episodes (in narratives).

Look for connections. Look for repeated words or repeated themes. Look for logical connections like cause-and-effect. Be sure to note the conjunctions between the paragraphs. In narrative episodes pay attention to the time sequence of each episode. And remember — keep looking and keep digging and keep reading and, whatever you do, don't stop after one short glance at the text. Immerse yourself in the passage. Search for these connections. They are critical to the meaning.

10. Story Shifts: Major Breaks and Pivots

As you read larger units of text, look for critical places where the story seems to take a new turn. In the letters this takes the form of a *major break*. The writer will shift topics, frequently changing from doctrinal discussion to practical discussion. These *shifts* are important to note. These *shifts* occur in narrative also, but they usually take the form of *pivot episodes*. Usually a shift in the direction of the story will be signaled by an unusually significant episode (a *pivot episode*).

For example, in the first three chapters of Paul's letter to the Ephesians, he presents a doctrinal explanation about the Ephesians' new life in Christ and the implications of that new life, especially regarding the unity of Jews and Gentiles in that new life. Ephesians 4:1, however, signals a *major break*, because Paul now begins to give practical exhortations about how the Ephesians ought to put the doctrine of chapters 1–3 into practice. So while chapters 1–3 deal primarily with doctrine, chapters 4–6 focus on practical living.

Example

This example is from Colossians 1:3–8:

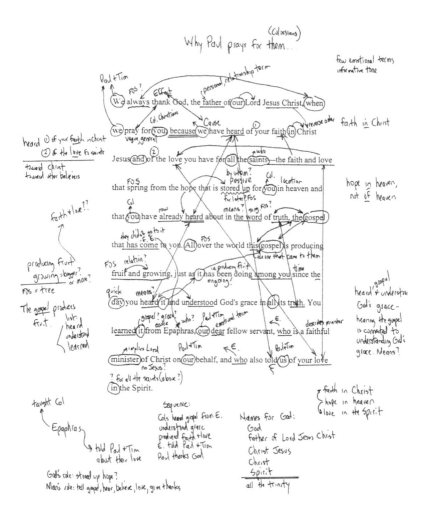

Conclusion

In order for us to interpret and understand the Bible, we must first read it carefully, observing all the details. We must observe it both at the sentence level and at larger levels like the paragraph and the episode. We have listed some features to look for — cause-and-effect, repetition, general-to-specific, and so on. This list is far from exhaustive. The purpose of the features we have listed is to get you started into careful reading. We have presented some of the major literary features to look for. But as you are finding out, reading carefully — really observing closely — involves looking at all the details and asking numerous questions of the text.

Keep in mind that we are still only at the first step in our journey into God's Word. Later we will move on to determining the meaning and applying the meaning. Chapters 2 and 3 about observation and careful reading, however, are critical, because if you bypass the careful reading step and move straight to application after only a superficial reading, you will almost certainly miss the meaning of the passage. In addition, the Bible will become boring for you because you will never see anything in it that you haven't already seen. If you read carefully, however, and observe, observe, observe, you will be much more likely to arrive at the true meaning and the Bible will become interesting to you because you will be seeing new things.

Because it is God's Word, the Bible is a unique piece of literature. It is like a mine that never plays out. One can dig in it for a lifetime and not exhaust it. Both of us have been studying the Bible seriously for over twenty-five years, yet we continue to see new things — new insights that we never noticed, new connections we never made. This keeps the Bible fresh and exciting for us. Our hope and prayer for you is that you will continue to read God's Word carefully and study the text with discipline. Make this a lifelong pursuit. The rewards are rich.

Discussion Questions

1. Why do you think it is important to observe both the details of a text (chapter 2) and the larger patterns within a text (chapter 3)?

2. Besides what is listed for observation in chapters 2 and 3, what other characteristics of a passage do you find it helpful to observe?

3. What are the benefits of careful observation? What happens if the interpreter does nothing more than observe?

Writing Assignment

Photocopy Philippians 2:1–4 below. Try following the example on page 39, making observations on this passage. Write down as many observations as you can. Write in the text and in the margins.

[1]If you have any encouragement from being united with Christ, if any

comfort from his love, if any fellowship with the Spirit, if any tenderness

and compassion, [2]then make my joy complete by being like-minded, hav-

ing the same love, being one in spirit and purpose. [3]Do nothing out of

selfish ambition or vain conceit, but in humility consider others better

than yourselves. [4]Each of you should look not only to your own interests,

but also to the interests of others.

What Do *We* Bring to the Text? 4

*I*n the next two chapters we will be discussing the importance of *context* to biblical interpretation. One context that is often overlooked is the context of the reader—the world from which the reader approaches the text. As readers of the Bible, we are not by nature neutral and objective. We bring a lot of preconceived notions and influences with us to the text when we read. Thus, we need to discuss and evaluate these "pretext" influences, lest they mislead us in our search for the meaning of the text.

Preunderstanding

One major influence that can skew our interpretive process and lead us away from the real meaning in the text is what we call *preunderstanding*. Preunderstanding refers to all of our preconceived notions and understandings that we bring to the text, which have been formulated, both consciously and subconsciously, *before* we actually study the text in detail. The preunderstanding problem is the broader issue that links with the cultural problems discussed in more detail below. Preunderstanding includes specific experiences and previous encounters with the text that tend to make us assume that we already understand it.

Preunderstanding is formed by both good and bad influences, some accurate and some inaccurate. It includes everything you have heard in Sunday school, at church, in Bible studies, and in your private reading of the Bible. However, preunderstandings of biblical texts are also formed by hymns and other Christian music, pop songs, jokes, art, and nonbiblical literature, both Christian and secular. Likewise, culture constantly creeps in.

Another dangerous aspect of preunderstanding surfaces when we come to the text with a theological agenda already formulated. That is, we start into a text with a specific slant we are looking for, and we use the text merely to search for details that fit with our agenda. Anything that does not fit in with the meaning we are looking for we simply skip or ignore. That is, *we* as readers stand *over* the Word of God and determine what it means, rather than placing ourselves *under* that Word, seeking diligently to determine what *God* means in the text.

A related danger is that of familiarity. If we are thoroughly familiar with a passage, we tend to think that we know all there is to know about it and are prone to skip over it without studying it carefully. Hopefully you realized in chapters 2 and 3 that most passages have a lot of depth to them, and we are unlikely to exhaust them or to grasp all there is to grasp in a few short visits to that text. Familiarity with a passage creates preunderstanding. As we revisit these familiar texts, we must resist the temptation of letting our familiarity dictate our conclusions before we even get started studying a text.

One of the most powerful, yet subtle, aspects of preunderstanding is that of culture. Our theology tells us to ask, *What would Jesus do?* Our culture, however, may subconsciously be telling us to ask, *What would Jason Bourne do?* Undoubtedly, our culture has a tremendous influence on how we read and interpret the Bible. For example, even though we believe that Jesus is our Lord and Savior, when he tells us to turn the other cheek, a voice in the back of our head objects. After all, turning the other cheek is not really the American way. It is not what Jason Bourne would do. Perhaps he might turn his cheek once and let his adversary strike him a second time just to demonstrate his patience and control, but undoubtedly after that second strike he would thrash the bad guy soundly (and we would all cheer). None of our action heroes turns the other cheek!

Thus, when we read of such a command from Jesus, we immediately try to interpret it in such a way that it does not conflict with cultural norms, especially those set by the culture's heroes. This culture-driven predisposition we call *cultural baggage*. Imagine that you are about to embark on a long hike in the mountains on a hot day. You wear good hiking boots and a hat. You bring sunglasses and a canteen. Should you bring three or four suitcases along? How ridiculous! Can you imagine hiking through the mountains with a suitcase under each arm?

If we are not careful, our culture will likewise weigh us down on the Interpretive Journey and hinder us from discovering God's message to us. Our culture tends to make us skew the text as we read it, twisting it to fit with our cultural world. Or, sometimes our culture works in us subconsciously to fill in all the gaps and missing details of the passage we are reading.

A good illustration of the subconscious influence of culture on our preunderstanding occurs when we read the book of Jonah and then try to visualize Jonah inside the great fish. Try to imagine this scene yourself. What do you see? Do you see Jonah squashed-up inside of the tight stomach of a whale, with no space between him and the stomach walls? Most people do not see that image. Many people, including ourselves, see Jonah inside a circular-shaped stomach, about six to eight feet in diameter, with a little bit of water at the bottom. Obviously this is not really what the inside of a whale (or fish) looks like.

So why do we see this? Where might this image come from? We suggest it comes from the movie (or book) *Pinocchio*. In this Walt Disney movie a whale swallows the main character, Pinocchio. The movie then presents us with a scene that portrays Pinocchio sitting inside the whale (a barrel-shaped room on its side, six to eight feet in diameter, etc.). This movie thus leaves us with a subconscious image of a person sitting inside a whale. When we read of Jonah's digestive misfortune, our minds begin an image search back through our memory banks, looking for a picture from which to visualize the event. As our mind searches through the files in its memory, it hits a match in the Pinocchio file, and a picture comes to mind without our conscious reckoning of where we obtained the image. Subconsciously we begin to fill in the descriptive gaps in the Jonah story with information that comes from a Hollywood movie! Thus, we find ourselves influenced in our reading of the Bible without even realizing what has happened. Cultural influence is huge!

What exactly do we mean by *culture?* Our culture is a combination of family and national heritage. You learn it from your Mom at breakfast, from the kids on the playground at school, and from television. It is a mix of language, customs, stories, movies, jokes, literature, and national habits. For Americans it is comprised of Big Macs, Barbie dolls, Tiger Woods, and Hollywood all mixed-in with George Washington, Babe Ruth, the Mississippi River, Walmart, and the space shuttle.

Cultural influences can vary somewhat, however, even within the same city. If you grew up in an inner city, blue-collar, Catholic home with both parents, your culture differs in many respects from someone who grew up in a suburban, white-collar, single-parent, Protestant home, but you will still share many of the same cultural influences. However, even though they share some common cultural features, black, white, Asian, and Hispanic cultures differ significantly, even within North America. Once you move out of North America, you will encounter even more drastic differences in culture.

Your family background is a central element in your cultural world. You have inherited many, many values, ideas, and images (for good and for bad) from your family. For example, what are your views about money, work, the poor, or the unemployed? Your views have undoubtedly been shaped by your family's socioeconomic setting and its outlook.

Your family also provides you with your strongest frame of reference regarding relationships. If you were fortunate enough to grow up in a loving, caring family, it will be easy for you to transpose the imagery of this experience to the imagery of God's care for you. If you had a loving father, for example, then the biblical image of God as a loving Father will be easy for you to grasp. In this case, the cultural influence of your family background helps you to grasp the biblical truth about God.

Unfortunately, however, not everyone has had a loving father. Those who have grown up with negligent or even abusive fathers carry a lot of baggage into the biblical texts that describe God as a Father. This doesn't mean that these people cannot grasp this aspect of biblical truth, but it does mean that they will have to work harder to overcome some of the negative images from their childhood. Other images of God and his care may relate better to them. As we all seek to understand God's Word, it is important that we acknowledge and identify the cultural influences at work in our heads and hearts.

We recognize full well that Christians do not culturally misread the Bible intentionally. As noted above, all of us tend to be influenced by our culture subconsciously. It is a natural thing to do, and we do it without thinking about it.

This subconscious interpretation, however, affects our understanding of the Bible in two ways. (1) We tend to fill in all of the gaps and ambiguities in the biblical texts with explanations and background from our culture. (2) More damaging to our interpretation is the fact that our cultural background preforms a parameter of limiting possibilities for a text even before we grapple with the intended meaning. In this situation, based on our culture we subconsciously create a world of interpretive possibilities and a world of interpretive impossibilities. In other words, our cultural setting has driven us to decide possible and impossible meanings for the text even before we study them.

Let's examine again Jesus' command to turn the other cheek. Our subconscious agenda seeks to legitimize our cultural worldview, that is, the way things are in our culture. Thus, before we even start to explore what Jesus meant when he said this, we place parameters of possibility around the text and eliminate culturally conflicting possible meanings. It cannot possibly mean that if someone bad hits you, you are to let them hit you again. However, by doing this we are placing our culture above the Bible and reading the Bible through culture-colored lenses. In this way we miss one of the main points of the Bible, namely, that the biblical message is from God and is above culture. The challenge is to critique our culture with the Bible and not vice versa.

Preunderstanding, including culture, is not inherently bad, but it can often skew our understanding of the Bible, leading us down the trail of misinterpretation. We do not want to abandon our preunderstanding, throwing all of our previous encounters with the text into the trash. What we do want to do is to submit our preunderstanding to the text, placing it under the text and not over the text. We must be able to identify our preunderstanding and then be open to changing it in accordance with a truly serious study of the text. That is, after we have studied the text thoroughly, we then evaluate our preunderstanding and modify it appropriately in light of our current study.

Biblical Presuppositions

Our approach to preunderstanding, however, does not suggest that our objective is to read and interpret the Bible in a completely neutral manner, apart from any presuppositional viewpoint, such as faith. Total objectivity is impossible for any reader of any text. Neither is it our goal. Striving for objectivity in biblical interpretation does not mean abandoning faith or trying to adopt the methods of unbelievers. Trying to read the Bible apart from faith does not produce objectivity.

We define preunderstanding and biblical presupposition as two distinct entities that we deal with in two quite different ways. We must let our preunderstanding change each time we study a passage. We submit it to the text and then interact with it, evaluate it in light of our study, and, one would hope, improve it each time. Biblical presuppositions, by contrast, do not change with each reading. They are not related to particular passages but to our overall view of the Bible.

As Christians we serve the living Lord and have the Holy Spirit living within us. The relationship we have with God is a critical aspect of the communication we have with him through reading his Word. This relationship impacts us greatly as we interpret, and it is not something we want to renegotiate each time we read a text, as we do with preunderstanding aspects. Rather, it is something we want to use. It is important to note that we as evangelical Christians have several *presuppositions* about the Bible itself that develop out of our relationship with Christ that we will not set aside when we tackle a passage. For example:

1. The Bible is the Word of God. Although God worked through people to produce it, it is nonetheless inspired by the Holy Spirit and is God's Word to us.
2. The Bible is trustworthy and true.
3. God has entered into human history; thus the supernatural (miracles, etc.) does occur.

4. The Bible is not contradictory; it is unified, yet diverse. Nevertheless, God is bigger than we are, and he is not always easy to comprehend. Thus, the Bible also has tension and mystery to it.

We could perhaps add other presuppositions, but these are the central ones that need to be mentioned in this chapter. These presuppositions have to do with how we view the entire Bible and serve as foundations on which to build our method of study.

Conclusion — Can We Be Objective?

Many writers have pointed out that total objectivity in interpretation is impossible, and we acknowledge this. However, total objectivity is not our goal. As Christians who have an intimate relationship with God through Jesus Christ, we are not striving for a neutral, objective viewpoint. We do not seek to be secular historians as we study the text (they are not objective either). We seek to hear what God has to say to us. Thus, we approach the text through faith and in the Spirit. So we want objectivity within the framework of evangelical presuppositions like those listed above. This type of objectivity has to do with preventing *our* preunderstanding, *our* culture, *our* familiarity, or *our* laziness from obscuring the meaning God intends for us in the text.

This task also can be challenging; however, it is to this task that *Journey into God's Word* is devoted. Every chapter in this book deals with some aspect of correcting our preunderstanding or neutralizing the negative cultural influences on our understanding. The observation tools we learned in chapters 2 and 3 will help us to be objective. The method of reading carefully that was presented in those chapters requires that we submit our preunderstanding to the text while we scrutinize it for details. Merely discovering the details of the text often corrects many of our preunderstandings and cultural misconstruals.

This chapter has merely delineated the problems we as readers bring to the text — the cultural baggage and preunderstandings that we must deal with as pre-text issues. The solution to the problem lies within the Interpretive Journey. We hope you are finding the trip rewarding. We certainly think it is worth all of the hard work and effort that you must exert as you travel through the following chapters!

Discussion Questions

1. What is the difference between preunderstanding and presuppositions as defined in this chapter?
2. How do you think your own preunderstanding influences the way you read the Bible?
3. How should we deal with our preunderstanding as we go about the task of responsible interpretation?

Writing Assignment

Describe your family background in regard to cultural influences. Discuss as well as you can both your mother (and her family) and your father (and his family). Include any other families that may have influenced you as well. For each, discuss attitudes and views toward religion, family, work, education, and wealth. Describe the socioeconomic location of your family and its religious context. Also, how do members of your family tend to relate to each other? Does your family tend to be warm and huggy or cold and distant? Finally, try to relate your family background to your own set of values and outlooks. What have you retained? What have you rejected?

Discovering the Historical-Cultural Context

5

We believe that the way we approach the Bible (i.e., the way we listen to God) should match how God gave us the Bible (i.e., the way God chose to speak). Otherwise, we will likely misunderstand what God is trying to say to us. Since God spoke his message in specific, historical situations (i.e., to people living in particular places, speaking particular languages, adopting a particular way of life), we should take the ancient situation seriously.

The bottom line is that we cannot simply ignore "those people living back then" and jump directly to what God wants to say to us. Why not? Again, because the way we listen to God (our interpretive approach) must honor the way God chose to communicate. We should not be so arrogant and prideful as to think that God cared nothing about the original audience but was merely using them to get a message to us.

The truth of the matter is that God cared deeply about the original hearers and spoke to them within their own historical-cultural situation. God also cares deeply about us and wants to speak to us. The time-bound message of Scripture contains eternally relevant principles that we can discover and apply to our lives. Remember that the Interpretive Journey moves from the meaning of the text for the biblical audience across the river of differences (e.g., time, place, culture, situation) by means of the principlizing bridge to the application of those theological principles in our lives.

Thus, we need to know the original historical-cultural context because it offers us a window into what God was saying to the biblical audience. Since we live in a different context, we must first recapture the meaning of the text in its original context. Then we can apply it to our lives in ways that will be just as relevant. God's Word is eternally relevant. Our task as students of his Word is to discover that relevance by doing our contextual homework.

This leads us to a crucial interpretive principle: For our interpretation of any biblical text to be valid, it must be consistent with the historical-cultural context of that text.[2] If our interpretation would not have made sense back then, we are probably on the wrong track. We must first determine what a text meant "in their town" before we can determine what it means and how we should apply that meaning to our own time and culture. Our *goal*, then, is to understand the historical-cultural context of the biblical passage as clearly as possible in order to grasp the meaning of the passage. In this chapter you will learn about the historical-cultural context (commonly referred to as "background"). In the next chapter you will discover more about literary context.

What Is Historical-Cultural Context?

By *historical-cultural context* we are referring to information about the biblical writer, the biblical audience, and any other historical-cultural elements touched on by the passage itself. Historical-cultural context relates to just about anything outside the text that will help you understand the text itself (e.g., what life was like for the Israelites as they wandered in the desert, what the Pharisees believed about the Sabbath, where Paul was when he wrote Philippians). Literary context, by contrast, relates to the context within the book (e.g., the form a passage takes, the flow of argument within the book, and the meaning of the words and sentences that surround the passage you are studying). Let's look briefly at each aspect of historical-cultural context and mention a few resources you can use to uncover that context.

The Biblical Writer

Because God chose to work through human authors as the immediate source of his inspired Word, the more we know about the human author the better. Try to find out as much as you can about the writer's background. Try to determine when he wrote and the kind of ministry he had (e.g., Hosea's ministry was linked to his marriage to his infamous wife, Gomer). You will also want to understand more about the specific relationship between the writer and the people he was addressing (e.g., note Paul's stern tone in his letter to the Galatians, but his praise for the Thessalonians).

Perhaps the most important thing to know about the biblical writers is why they are writing. Why does the author of 1 and 2 Chronicles, for example, repeat much of Samuel and Kings? The answer lies in the writer's purpose. The Chronicler (perhaps Ezra) is writing for Israel *after* the Exile (i.e., for the restored community). He is trying to show that God is still very much interested in his people after judging them by the Exile. For example, the Chronicler seems to idealize David and Solomon by omitting anything that might tarnish their image (e.g., David's sin with Bathsheba). In this way the writer reassures his audience that although God has judged his people, he still loves them and wants to use them to accomplish his purposes. So, when it comes to the biblical writer, try to determine his background, the time of writing, the kind of ministry he was seeking to fulfill, his relationship with the people he addresses, and why he is writing.

The Biblical Audience

Discovering the historical-cultural context also involves knowing something about the biblical audience and their circumstances. Take Mark's Gospel as an example. Mark makes a point of emphasizing the cross of Christ and the demands of discipleship throughout his Gospel. Many scholars believe that Mark's original audience was the church in the vicinity of Rome and that Mark was preparing them for the persecution they would soon face at the hands of Emperor Nero during the mid-60s AD. To encourage these believers to remain faithful in the midst of suffering, Mark stresses how Jesus remained faithful during his time of suffering.

Other Historical-Cultural Elements

As noted earlier, historical-cultural context involves the biblical writer and the biblical audience, plus any historical-cultural elements touched upon by your passage. Sometimes it is difficult to know much about the biblical author and the audience or their specific circumstances. Often you will focus more on the historical, social, religious, political, and economic elements that shape your passage. Here are a few examples of how understanding these elements can shed light on the meaning of your passage.

Sometimes knowing more about the geography or topography assumed by the text can help you grasp its meaning. Jesus starts his parable of the good Samaritan with the statement: "A man was going down from Jerusalem to Jericho" (Luke 10:30). You would certainly go down from Jerusalem to Jericho, descending from about 2,500 feet above sea level to about 800 feet below sea level. In addition, the trip would not be a walk in the park. The distance is almost twenty miles and would take you through some rugged desert country that offered plenty of hiding places for thieves. Knowing the geography helps you understand how easy it would have been to pass by the dying man and how troublesome it would have been to be a loving neighbor.

One of the most productive areas of background study relates to social customs. If you are studying Ephesians 5:21–6:9, for example, you need to know something about Greco-Roman household codes in order to make sense of your passage. These rules were developed primarily to instruct the head of the household about how to deal with members of his family. The apostle Paul uses the household code concept, but he transforms it in powerful ways. For instance, Greco-Roman codes told husbands to make their wives submit, but they never listed love as a duty of the husband. In Ephesians 5:25 Paul breaks the mold when he instructs husbands to "love your wives, just as Christ loved the church and gave himself up for her." Paul's exhortation for all members of the household to "submit to one another out of reverence for Christ" (5:21) would have been even more radical.

Sometimes your passage will touch on economic issues. On his second missionary tour (Acts 15:39–18:22), Paul plants a church at Philippi. There Paul and Silas meet a slave girl who has a spirit by which she predicts the future. She continues to bother the missionary team until Paul finally commands the spirit to come out of her. Her enraged owners then drag Paul and Silas into the marketplace, where the magistrates order them to be stripped, beaten, and later imprisoned for causing trouble. All this happens because the demon-possessed slave girl has been earning a lot of money for her owners. When the spirit left the girl, the money left the owners' pockets, and they take their revenge on the missionaries.

You also need to pay attention to political issues that may surface in your passage. In the Acts 16 episode notice what happens next to Paul and Silas. After spending time in prison (where God does some exciting things), the magistrates send word that the missionaries may leave the city (Acts 16:36–40). Since it was illegal to publicly beat and imprison a Roman citizen, especially without a trial, the Roman officials act quickly to apologize for their actions. Paul and Silas probably demand an escort out of town in order to make a public statement about their innocence for the benefit of the church in Philippi.

Historical-cultural context includes information about the author and the audience—their background, circumstances, and relationship—as well as geographical, social, religious, economic, and political elements connected to the passage. Some people are convinced that background studies are tedious ways of making the Bible less relevant. We have found the opposite to be true. When we take time to understand the context, the passage comes alive and explodes with relevance (sometimes more than we can take). We are able to see that God was speaking to real people struggling with real life and that he continues to speak to us.

Before citing various resources one can use to study the historical-cultural context, we want to mention a few of the dangers associated with studying this type of material.

Dangers Associated with Studying Background

While the greatest danger is ignoring the historical-cultural context, there are also dangers associated with studying it. To begin with, you need to *watch out for inaccurate background information*. For example, those who say that the "eye of a needle" in Matthew 19:23–24 refers to the "camel's gate" in Jerusalem are likely mistaken. There is no evidence for this kind of gate and the "eye of a needle" meant essentially what it means today (i.e., the eye of a sewing needle). Jesus is using the largest animal in Palestine and one of the smallest openings to make a forceful statement about how hard it is for the rich and powerful to enter God's kingdom.

A second danger associated with studying historical-cultural context is that of elevating the background of the text above the meaning of the text. When studying the parable of the Pharisee and the tax collector in Luke 18:9–14, for instance, you may be tempted to spend all your time learning about Pharisees and tax collectors. You certainly need to know something about these two groups and their role and reputation in Jesus' day. Yet you don't want to let your fascination with background information cause you to miss the point—God judges the proud and exalts the humble.

Finally, we caution you not to let yourself slowly evolve into nothing more than a walking database of ancient facts. Don't lose your interpretive heart in your quest for information to deepen your understanding of the text. Keep your study of the background of the Bible in proper perspective. We study the historical-cultural context not as an end in itself, but as a tool to help us grasp and apply the meaning of the biblical text.

The Historical-Cultural Context of the Whole Book

To identify the historical-cultural context you need to (1) grasp the historical-cultural context of *the book* that contains your passage and (2) recognize the specific historical-cultural context of *the passage* itself.

In order to understand the historical-cultural context of the entire book, we suggest you consult Bible handbooks, introductions, and surveys of the Old and New Testaments, and especially good commentaries.

Bible Handbooks

These resources usually begin with general articles about the Bible and the world of the Bible (e.g., the nature of Scripture, life in Bible times). They normally include a brief introduction to each book of the Bible and an equally brief running commentary on the entire biblical text. We have found the following Bible handbooks useful:

Alexander, Pat, and David Alexander, eds. *Zondervan Handbook to the Bible*. Grand Rapids: Zondervan, 1999.

Dockery, David S., ed. *Holman Bible Handbook*. Nashville: Holman, 1992.

Thompson, J. A. *Handbook of Life in Bible Times*. Downers Grove, IL: InterVarsity Press, 1986.

Old and New Testament Introductions and Surveys

These tools supply detailed background information on each book as well as an overview of the book's contents. Usually they discuss authorship, date, recipients, situation, purpose, and more. Generally speaking, introductions offer more technical discussions of the background issues and spend less time on the actual content of the books, while surveys touch on background issues and focus more on content. These types of books normally go into greater detail than Bible handbooks, so there is simply too much information to fit both Old Testament and New Testament into a single volume. Here are a few of the better ones:

Arnold, Bill, and Bryan Beyer. *Encountering the Old Testament*. Grand Rapids: Baker, 1999.

Carson, D. A., and Douglas J. Moo. *An Introduction to the New Testament*. 2nd ed. Grand Rapids: Zondervan, 2005.

Dillard, Raymond B., and Tremper Longman III. *An Introduction to the Old Testament*. 2nd edition. Grand Rapids: Zondervan, 2006.

Elwell, Walter, and Robert Yarbrough. *Encountering the New Testament*. Grand Rapids: Baker, 1998.

Gundry, Robert H. *A Survey of the New Testament*. 4th ed. Grand Rapids: Zondervan, 2003.

LaSor, William S., David Alan Hubbard, and Frederic W. Bush. *Old Testament Survey*. 2nd ed. Grand Rapids: Eerdmans, 1996.

Walton, John H., and Andrew E. Hill. *Old Testament Today*. Grand Rapids: Zondervan, 2004.

Commentaries

In most cases a good commentary will be your best bet for up-to-date, detailed information about the historical-cultural context of the book that contains your passage. Because commentaries are always written from a particular point of view and since they differ in quality and scope, it is always a good idea to consult more than one commentary. We recommend that you consult a commentary in one of the following series as you begin your study. There are certainly other fine commentaries (and some are not attached to a series), but this is a solid place to start.

> Baker Exegetical Commentary. Grand Rapids: Baker.
> Bible Speaks Today. Downers Grove, IL: InterVarsity Press.
> Expositor's Bible Commentary. Grand Rapids: Zondervan.
> IVP New Testament Commentary. Downers Grove, IL: InterVarsity Press.
> New American Commentary. Nashville: Broadman & Holman.
> New International Commentary on the New Testament. Grand Rapids: Eerdmans.
> New International Commentary on the Old Testament. Grand Rapids: Eerdmans.
> NIV Application Commentary. Grand Rapids: Zondervan.
> Pillar New Testament Commentaries. Grand Rapids: Eerdmans.
> Tyndale New Testament Commentaries. Downers Grove, IL: InterVarsity Press.
> Tyndale Old Testament Commentaries. Downers Grove, IL: InterVarsity Press.

The Historical-Cultural Context of the Passage

After you have a good sense of the background of the book that contains your passage, you need to identify the historical-cultural context of the passage itself. This involves examining any elements of history and culture that are connected to or mentioned in the passage (e.g., geography, politics, religion, economics, family life, social customs). To accomplish this, we recommend using Bible atlases, Bible dictionaries or encyclopedias, commentaries, background commentaries, Old and New Testament histories, and special studies on ancient life and culture.

Bible Atlases

If you want to learn more about the people, places, and events mentioned in your passage, take a look at a Bible atlas. You will find colorful maps of the land, pictures of many of the important sites, helpful charts of political and religious leaders, discussions of the various periods of biblical history, and more. Here is a list of helpful Bible atlases:

Beitzel, Barry J. *The Moody Atlas of the Bible Lands.* Chicago: Moody, 1985.

Brisco, Thomas C. *Holman Bible Atlas.* Nashville: Broadman & Holman, 1998.

Lawrence, Paul, ed. *The IVP Atlas of Bible History.* Downers Grove, IL: InterVarsity, 2006.

Rasmussen, Carl G. *Zondervan NIV Atlas of the Bible.* Grand Rapids: Zondervan, 1989.

Bible Dictionaries and Encyclopedias

This is the place to go when you need information about a particular topic mentioned in your passage. For instance, if you want to know more about the garden of Gethsemane, consult a Bible dictionary or encyclopedia. These resources cover a full range of biblical topics and arrange the topics alphabetically. All you have to do is turn to "Gethsemane" and read. Included among the most helpful Bible dictionaries and encyclopedias for the beginning student are the following:

Butler, Trent, Chad Brand, Charles W. Draper, and Archie England, eds. *Holman Illustrated Bible Dictionary.* Nashville: Broadman & Holman, 2003.

Douglas, J. D., ed. *The Illustrated Bible Dictionary.* 3 vols. Downers Grove, IL: InterVarsity Press, 1980.

Douglas, J. D., and Merrill C. Tenney, eds. *New International Bible Dictionary.* Grand Rapids: Zondervan, 1987.

Elwell, Walter. *Baker Encyclopedia of the Bible.* 2 vols. Grand Rapids: Baker, 1988.

Hays, J. Daniel, J. Scott Duvall, and C. Marvin Pate. *The Dictionary of Biblical Prophecy and the End Times.* Grand Rapids: Zondervan, 2007.

Marshall, I. Howard, A. R. Millard, J. I. Packer, and D. J. Wiseman, eds. *New Bible Dictionary.* 3rd ed. Downers Grove, IL: InterVarsity Press, 1996.

Reid, Daniel G., ed. *The IVP Dictionary of the New Testament.* Downers Grove, IL: InterVarsity Press, 2004.

Commentaries and Background Commentaries

We mention commentaries again because the good ones are also helpful in shedding light on background matters within your specific passage. Do you recall Paul's harsh words for the Corinthian Christians regarding their practice of celebrating the Lord's Supper (see 1 Corinthians 11:17–22)? A good commentary will do what Craig Blomberg does in his commentary on 1 Corinthians — it will clarify the meaning of the passage by summarizing the historical-cultural context.

> The minority of well-to-do believers (1:26), including the major financial supporters and owners of the homes in which the believers met, would have had the leisure-time and resources to arrive earlier and bring larger quantities and finer food than the rest of the congregation. Following the practice of hosting festive gatherings in ancient Corinth, they would have quickly filled the small private dining room. Latecomers (the majority, who probably had to finish work before coming on Saturday or Sunday evening — there was as of yet no legalized day off in the Roman empire) would be seated separately in the adjacent atrium or courtyard. Those that could not afford to bring a full meal, or a very good one, did not have the opportunity to share with the rest in the way that Christian unity demanded....
>
> The result of the lack of consideration by the wealthy for the less well-to-do implies that they are not celebrating the *Lord's* Supper at all, merely "their *own* supper."[3]

A relatively new type of commentary is called the background commentary. These resources focus not on the meaning of each passage but on historical-cultural background essential to grasping the meaning. Background commentaries are helpful because they provide a wealth of information conveniently arranged in a verse-by-verse format. As you study Jesus' teaching on nonresistance in Matthew 5, you will come across the statement: "And if someone wants to sue you and take your tunic, let him have your cloak as well" (v. 40). Keener's background commentary offers the following insight into the context of the passage:

> The poorest people of the Empire (e.g., most peasants in Egypt) had only an inner and outer garment, and the theft of a cloak would lead to legal recourse. Although conditions in first-century Palestine were not quite that bad, this verse could indicate divestiture of all one's possessions, even (hyperbolically) one's clothes, to avoid a legal dispute affecting only oneself. Jesus gives this advice in spite of the fact that, under Jewish law, a legal case to regain one's cloak would have been foolproof: a creditor could not take a poor person's outer cloak, which might serve as one's only blanket at night as well as a coat (Ex 22:26–27).[4]

It's hard to overestimate the value of the following background commentaries:

Arnold, Clint. *Zondervan Illustrated Bible Background Commentary.* 4 vols. Grand Rapids: Zondervan, 2002.

Keener, Craig S. *The IVP Bible Background Commentary: New Testament.* Downers Grove, IL: InterVarsity Press, 1993.

Walton, John H., Victor H. Matthews, and Mark W. Chavalas. *The IVP Bible Background Commentary: Old Testament.* Downers Grove, IL: InterVarsity Press, 2000.

Computer Software and Internet Resources

You will be able to find some of the resources we have mentioned above in electronic format. We encourage you to take full advantage of computer software packages that include the best resources. Often the convenience and price are hard to beat. But remember that you are after the best tools, not simply the least expensive deal. You can use the bibliography of resources throughout this chapter to evaluate the various software packages.

You need to be much more cautious about Internet resources. This is a rapidly changing environment that has not traditionally represented the best in biblical scholarship. While the Internet is certainly convenient, you don't always know whether you are getting reliable information. We recommend that you stick with articles by respected authors.

Conclusion

In this chapter we have learned about the importance of historical-cultural context in the process of interpreting and applying the Bible. We cannot overemphasize the importance of context for faithfully reading Scripture. Remember, we study the historical-cultural background of the Bible because God chose to speak first to ancient peoples living in cultures that are radically different from our own. As we recapture the original context of God's Word, we will be able to grasp its meaning and apply that meaning to our lives.

While some may label background studies "boring" and "irrelevant," we argue just the opposite — that knowing the background of a passage can clarify its meaning and heighten our understanding of its relevance. We believe that studying the historical-cultural context of a passage is among the most practical things you can do when it comes to Bible study.

Discussion Questions

1. What can happen when people approach the Bible without any concern for the historical-cultural context? Care to share any examples from your own experience?
2. Can you think of an example of the historical-cultural context shedding significant light on the meaning of a biblical text?
3. For people living in an "instant application" society such as ours, what can persuade them to put forth effort to study the historical-cultural context?

Writing Assignment

Read the conversation between Jesus and the Samaritan woman recorded in John 4:1 – 39. Then read an article on "Samaria" or "Samaritan" in a Bible dictionary or encyclopedia and make a list of all the ways the information helps you understand the conversation between Jesus and the woman.

Discovering the Literary Context   6

*I*magine that you are a college student strolling to class one day when a total stranger hits you with a one-liner: "Go for it!" How would you respond? Would you say, "Sure," and walk away thinking that he or she was one fry short of a Happy Meal? Or would you take the message with all religious seriousness and conclude God must be speaking to you through that person, answering your prayers about your decision regarding a major, a new relationship, or whether to take the summer job?

To unveil the meaning of "go for it," most of us would probably come back with a few questions of our own. "What exactly do you mean?" or "Go for what?" We would ask questions as part of our search for a context to give meaning to those three little words. Without a context, "go for it" can mean almost anything. Without a context, words become meaningless.

When it comes to interpreting and applying the Bible, context is crucial. In fact, we would go so far as to say that the most important principle of biblical interpretation is that *context determines meaning*. When we ignore the context, we can twist the Scriptures and "prove" almost anything. Consider the example of a young man seeking advice from God's Word about whether to ask his girlfriend to marry him. As he dances around the Scriptures, he finds a couple of verses that provide the answer he so desperately wants with a timetable to boot.

1 Corinthians 7:36c: "They should get married."
John 13:27: "What you are about to do, do quickly."

The young man sees in the first verse a direct command to get married and in the second a timetable — get married now! God has spoken!

What keeps us from taking this ridiculous example seriously? *Context!* Apparently the young man did not bother to read the entire context of 1 Corinthians 7:36c, where the apostle Paul gives advice to engaged men in light of the distressing circumstances in Corinth (notice the italicized portions [italics have been added]):

> If anyone thinks he is acting improperly toward the virgin he is engaged to, and if she is getting along in years and he feels he ought to marry, he should do as he wants. He is not sinning. *They should get married.* But the man who has settled the matter in his own mind, who is under no compulsion but has control over his own will, and who has made up his mind not to marry the virgin — this man also does the right thing. *So then, he who marries the virgin does right, but he who does not marry her does even better.* (1 Corinthians 7:36 – 38)

In light of the situation, Paul actually says that it's better not to marry. In the second verse (John 13:27), the phrase "what you are about to do" refers to Judas's betraying Jesus and has nothing at all to do with marriage. Under the spotlight of context, we see that these two verses give the young man no scriptural basis for proposing marriage.

Not all examples are this ridiculous, of course, but every violation of context is a dangerous matter. By honoring the context of Scripture, we are saying that we would rather hear what God has to say than put words in his mouth. Context determines meaning!

Along with knowing more about the historical-cultural context, we also need to know about the literary context. *Literary context* relates to the particular form a passage takes (the *literary genre*) and to the words, sentences, and paragraphs that surround the passage you are studying (the *surrounding context*).

What Is Literary Genre?

Of every passage of Scripture, we must first notice the form it takes before we look at its content, since form affects content. The word *genre* is a word of French origin meaning "form" or "kind." When applied to biblical interpretation, the expression *literary genre* simply refers to the different *types* of literature found in the Bible. In the Old Testament you will encounter narrative, law, poetry, prophecy, and wisdom. The New Testament forms include gospel, history, letter, and prophetic-apocalyptic literature. Both Old and New Testaments feature a number of subgenres (e.g., parables, riddles, speeches).

Many linguists use the analogy of a game to describe literary genre. You can think of each genre as a different kind of game complete with its own set of rules. This insightful analogy shows how we as readers have to play by the rules when it comes to recognizing literary genre.

> Think for a moment of a European soccer fan attending his first (American) football and basketball games. In football the offensive and defensive players can use their hands to push their opponents. In basketball and soccer they cannot. In basketball players cannot kick the ball, but they can hold it with their hands. In soccer the reverse is true. In football everyone can hold the ball with his hands but only one person can kick it. In soccer everyone can kick the ball but only one person can hold it. Unless we understand the rules under which the game is played, what is taking place is bound to be confusing.
>
> In a similar way, there are different "game" rules involved in the interpretation of the different kinds of biblical literature. The author has "played his game"—that is, has sought to convey his meaning—under the rules covering the particular literary form he has used. Unless we know those rules, we will almost certainly misinterpret his meaning.[5]

For communication to occur, the reader must be on the same page as the author in terms of genre. When the stranger said "go for it," you could have responded with questions to clarify the meaning. But how can we clarify the meaning of the ancient authors when they are not around to field our questions? The answer is literary genre. Even though the author and reader cannot have a face-to-face conversation, they meet in the text where they are able to communicate because they subscribe to a common set of rules—the rules of the particular genre.

In this way, literary genre acts as a kind of *covenant of communication*, a fixed agreement between author and reader about how to communicate.[6]

In order for us to "keep the covenant," we must let the author's choice of genre determine the rules we use to understand his words. To disregard literary genre in the Bible is to violate our covenant with the biblical author and with the Holy Spirit who inspired his message.

If you stop and think about it, you are constantly encountering different genres in the course of ordinary life. In a single day you might read a newspaper, look up a number in a telephone directory, order from a menu, reflect on a poem, enjoy a love letter, read a map showing how to get to a friend's house, or meditate on a devotional book. When you meet these different genres, you know (whether conscious of it or not) that you need to play by certain rules of communication, the rules established by the genre itself. If you fail to play by their rules, you run the risk of misreading.

You run dangerous risks if you were to confuse a telephone directory with a love letter or mistake a menu for directions to a friend's house. Obviously we don't read menus the same way that we read love letters or newspapers the same way that we read devotional books. We know this because the genre game determines the rules for interpretation. Just as we know that the kind of game determines the rules we play by, so we know that each literary genre in the Bible comes with its own set of built-in rules for interpretation. When readers pay attention to those rules, they have a much greater chance of reading the passage as it was intended.

Genres shape our expectations about how to approach a particular text. The form or genre of the text really is connected to the content of the text, and for this reason, we should take literary genre seriously. The very meaning of the Bible is at stake!

What Is Surrounding Context?

Literary context includes not only the genre or type of literature, but also the *surrounding context*—the texts that surround the passage you are studying. You can think of it as the textual world in which your text lives. This includes the words, sentences, paragraphs, and discourses that come before and after your passage. The surrounding context of Romans 12:1–2, for instance, includes the first eleven chapters of Romans as well as Romans 12:3 through the end of the book. In a broader sense, the surrounding context of Romans 12:1–2 is the rest of the books in the New Testament and even the entire Old Testament. These various contexts form circles around your passage.

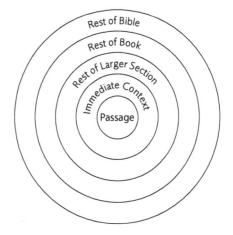

The *immediate context* circle is closest to the center since it describes what comes immediately before and after your passage. First Peter 5:7 is an encouraging verse: "Cast all your anxiety on him because he cares for you." Do you recall its immediate context? The immediate context includes at least verses 5–9, perhaps more (v. 7 has been put in bold, below).

Young men, in the same way be submissive to those who are older. All of you, clothe yourselves with humility toward one another, because,

"God opposes the proud
but gives grace to the humble."

Humble yourselves, therefore, under God's mighty hand, that he may lift you up in due time. **Cast all your anxiety on him because he cares for you.**

Be self-controlled and alert. Your enemy the devil prowls around like a roaring lion looking for someone to devour. Resist him, standing firm in the faith, because you know that your brothers throughout the world are undergoing the same kind of sufferings.

We encourage you to give highest priority to the immediate context when determining the meaning of your passage. As the circles of the context diagram illustrates, the closer the circle is to the center, the greater influence it usually has on the meaning of your passage.

A careful look at the immediate context of 1 Peter 5:7 reveals that casting our cares on the Lord is strongly tied to humbling ourselves before him. This relationship grows even stronger when we realize that the word "cast" (v. 7) is actually a participle in the Greek text and should be translated "casting" (see, e.g., the NASB translation).

The immediate context reveals that humbling ourselves before God means that we entrust our concerns and troubles to God because we know that God loves us and will not let us down. Pride says to God, "I can bear this burden by myself," whereas humility involves casting our cares on our caring God. What a positive definition of humility! And that insight comes from a careful reading of the immediate context.

The next step is learning to *identify* the surrounding context of your passage. Before we do that, however, we should first discuss a couple of dangers associated with disregarding context.

Dangers of Disregarding Literary Context

You have probably heard it said that you can make the Bible say anything you want. That is true *only* if you disregard the literary context. When you honor the literary context (including the covenant of communication implicit in the genre), you cannot make the Bible say just anything. Cults are famous for Scripture twisting, and most of their misreadings stem from a breach of literary context.[7] Just because we approach Scripture as evangelical Christians does not make us immune to misinterpretations should we decide to neglect literary context. There are a number of dangers associated with disregarding literary context. Here we will point out only two of the most common problems.

Ignoring the Surrounding Context

The first danger is simply ignoring the surrounding context. This usually happens when individuals focus on a single verse without paying attention to how the surrounding verses might affect its meaning. For example, do you know the context of 2 Timothy 2:22, which reads: "Flee the evil desires of youth, and pursue righteousness, faith, love and peace, along with those who call on the Lord out of a pure heart."

Second Timothy 2:22 is a favorite verse for fighting off sexual temptation. But how does the surrounding context define "evil desires of youth"? Paul is writing to Timothy, who is facing the problem of false teachers within the leadership of the church at Ephesus. The previous unit (2:14–19) makes it clear that Timothy must resist the false teachers. This is supported by an analogy from the household (2:20–21). Likewise, 2:23–26 speaks of false teaching. In verse 22 Paul tells Timothy to run away from foolish discussions, arguments, and theological novelties so attractive to young ministers (i.e., "evil desires of youth") and to run instead after righteousness, faith, love, and peace with the true people of God. Much to the surprise of some, this verse has little (if anything) to do with sexual temptation.

The way our Bibles have been divided into chapters and verses doesn't help matters much. The chapter and verse numbers help us find passages quickly, but they can also lead us to believe that each verse stands alone as an independent unit of thought, which is not the case. Just because we attach numbers to the sentences in a paragraph doesn't mean that we can rip one particular sentence out of its context and disconnect it from what precedes or follows.

We also need to remember that the chapter and verse divisions were not part of the original documents but were added much later. When we speak of the Holy Spirit's inspiring the Scriptures, we are talking about the text itself, not about the reference numbers. Don't let these later editorial additions cause you to lift individual sentences out of their surrounding context and give them a meaning never intended by their authors.

Topical Preaching

A second danger associated with disregarding literary context relates to how Scripture is preached. Topical preaching is a valid approach to preaching when the various passages are understood in context and the overall message doesn't violate those individual contexts. But far too often topical preaching distorts the meaning of Scripture by disregarding the literary context. Here is how that happens.

The diagram below shows how a biblical author's thought flows through a particular text. Expository preaching (in contrast to topical preaching) will follow an author's flow of thought through a particular text (e.g., John 10) in order to grasp the intended meaning and communicate that meaning to the congregation.

Topical preaching, by contrast, often jumps from one passage to another by stringing together a series of originally unrelated thoughts (see the resulting diagram below). That is the same as jumping from the newspaper to the menu to the poem to the love letter, picking thoughts at random, in order to construct a message of your own choosing. You can see how this approach could easily violate the literary context and lead to all sorts of unbiblical conclusions.

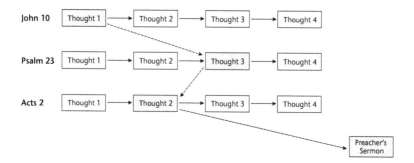

Quoting Bible passages out of context may make for an entertaining sermon, but it will mask God's true message. Misreading the Bible ultimately hurts people by enslaving them rather than setting them free with truth. What if the young man we mentioned at the beginning of the chapter really believed God had told him to marry his girlfriend when in fact God had done no such thing? The young man's failure to consider the context would cause a misreading with serious relational consequences. Of course, his girlfriend might say "no" to his proposal and encourage him to take a class on Interpreting the Bible. Then all would be well.

How to Identify the Surrounding Context

The Bible is more than a collection of unrelated parts. The Holy Spirit moved the biblical writers to connect their words, sentences, and paragraphs into a literary whole in the normal way that people use language to communicate. Just imagine how a document would appear if the sentences were not linked together to form a unified message. Better yet, read the following paragraph:

> I heard an interesting story on the news the other night. The quarterback faded back to pass. Carbon buildup was keeping the carburetor from functioning properly. The two-inch steaks were burned on the outside but raw on the inside. Ten-feet-high snow drifts blocked the road. The grass needed mowing. The elevator raced to the top of the one-hundred-story building in less than a minute. The audience booed the poor performance.[8]

We typically don't string together randomly selected ideas when we are trying to communicate. Normally, sentences build on previous sentences and lead into later sentences in order to produce a coherent message. As God's communication to us, the parts of the Bible connect to form a whole, while the whole in turn provides guidelines or boundaries for understanding the parts.

When we ask you to identify the surrounding context, we are asking you to see how these sentences (the parts) fit together in a book to communicate the larger message (the whole). We cannot read the author's mind, but we can trace his thought as it flows through each sentence and paragraph to form the whole book. We want to see how the smaller units connect to form the larger units. Moreover, the most accurate interpretation of a passage is the one that best fits that passage's surrounding context.

We are going to use the short New Testament book of Philemon to illustrate how you identify the surrounding context of a passage. Suppose that you are trying to determine the surrounding context of Philemon 4–7 (there is only one chapter in the entire book of Philemon). Take a moment and read Philemon in your Bible. To grasp what Paul really means in verses 4–7, you need to examine what Paul says before and after this passage. This is what we mean by "surrounding context"—how a section fits with what comes before and after it. Finding the surrounding context of any passage consists of three steps: identify how the book is divided into paragraphs or sections, summarize the main idea of each section, and explain how your particular passage relates to the surrounding sections. Let's continue with our Philemon example.

1. Identify how the book is divided into paragraphs or sections. Look at several different Bible translations to see how the translators have divided the book and the chapters into smaller units. Although there will not be universal agreement about how to divide the text into sections, often there will be a consensus among the translations (as there is with vv. 4–7). If you want to do the work yourself, you need to look for changes in the text as clues to a shift in the author's flow of thought (e.g., conjunctions, changes of literary type, topic or theme, time, location, setting). You will notice some of these transition points in Philemon. Paul switches from a greeting to a prayer between verses 3 and 4. Don't miss the conjunction "therefore" in verse 8 and the "so" in verse 17, both beginning new sections.

2. Summarize the main idea of each section in about a dozen words or less. For each statement that you write, make sure that you summarize the point of the whole section and not just a portion of the section. After writing a summary, you may want to read the section again and see if your summary truly captures the entire section. When writing your summary, think about two things: (a) the topic or main idea of the section, and (b) what the author says about the topic or main idea. Take a look at our summaries for each section of Philemon:

- vv. 1–3: Paul identifies the letter senders/recipients and offers a greeting.
- vv. 4–7: Paul thanks God for Philemon's faith and love and intercedes for him.
- vv. 8–16: Paul appeals to Philemon for his "son" Onesimus and offers Philemon perspective on God's providence in the matter.
- vv. 17–20: Paul urges Philemon to receive Onesimus as he would receive Paul himself.
- v. 21: Paul expresses confidence that Philemon will do even more than he asks.
- v. 22: Paul shares his hope to come in person and visit Philemon.
- vv. 23–24: Paul shares greetings from his fellow workers.
- v. 25: Paul closes the letter with a benediction of grace.

3. Explain how the section you are studying relates to the surrounding sections. Now that you can see the author's flow of thought through the entire book by reading your section summaries, it is time to look at how your passage fits into its surroundings. We tell our students, "If you do nothing else besides read what comes before and what comes after your passage, you will eliminate about 75 percent of all interpretive mistakes." The heart of identifying the surrounding context is observing how your section relates to what comes before it and what comes after it. In Philemon, our section (vv. 4–7) is sandwiched between the opening of the letter (vv. 1–3) and the body of the letter (vv. 8–22). Almost everything that Paul says in our thanksgiving and prayer passage prepares the reader for what he is about to say in the body of the letter.

In this case, the thanksgiving becomes the basis for the request that follows. Paul attributes a number of qualities to Philemon in verses 4–7, the very qualities that will enable him to respond positively to Paul's upcoming request. Paul thanks God that Philemon trusts the Lord and loves people. This love, Paul goes on to say, has "given me great joy and encouragement." He also commends Philemon for refreshing the hearts of the saints. Now Paul has a favor to ask about one saint in particular, Onesimus. Thus, the thanksgiving and prayer section (vv. 4–7) prepares the way for the body of the letter. Philemon's good qualities that are highlighted in verses 4–7 provide the character anchor that will motivate him to do what Paul is about to request in the rest of the letter. When we study Philemon 4–7 with its surrounding context in view, we can truly grasp the meaning of the passage.

Conclusion

We study literary context of Scripture because the interpretation that best fits the context is the most valid interpretation. When we disregard literary context, we run the risk of forcing the Bible to say what we want it to say. This may appear to satisfy people's immediate needs, but ultimately, this approach hurts people by robbing them of God's liberating truth. People are seeking time-tested answers to problems that are staring them in the face, answers that contemporary culture simply cannot supply. When we take the literary context seriously, we are saying, "We want to hear what God is trying to say to us."

We honor the literary context by playing by the game rules established by the author through his use of literary genre and when we pay close attention to the surrounding context. We ourselves communicate by connecting our words, sentences, and paragraphs into a coherent message, and the Bible does the same. As you honor the literary context of a passage of Scripture, you will be saying through your actions that above all, you want to hear what God has to say to you through his Word.

Discussion Questions

1. What happens if you carefully consider the surrounding context of a passage, but ignore its literary genre?
2. Besides those examples cited in this chapter, what are some instances of interpreting a biblical passage apart from its immediate context?
3. When is topical preaching contextually valid? When does it disregard and violate context?

Writing Assignment

Turn to the Old Testament book of Jonah and do the following:

1. Read the entire book of Jonah and identify how the book is divided into paragraphs or sections.
2. Summarize the main idea of each section in about a dozen words or less.
3. Explain how your particular passage (Jonah 1:13–16 for this exercise) relates to the surrounding context.

Which Bible Translation Should I Use?

7

*F*or your birthday you get some extra cash and you decide to buy a new Bible. The local Christian bookstore should have what you want. As you enter the store and turn the corner into the Bible section, you immediately notice a plethora of choices. You see *The Open Bible, The Thompson Chain Reference Study Bible, The NRSV Access Bible, The Life Application Study Bible, The NIV Study Bible, The Ryrie Study Bible, The NKJV Women's Study Bible, The KJV Promise Keepers Men's Study Bible, The Spirit-Filled Life Bible*, and about fifty other possibilities. You didn't know buying a new Bible could be so complicated. What should you do?

The first thing to know about selecting a Bible is that there is a big difference between the Bible version or translation and the format used by publishers to market the Bible. Packaging features such as study notes, introductory articles, and devotional insights are often helpful, but they are not part of the translation of the original text. When choosing a Bible, you will want to look past the marketing format to make sure you know which translation the Bible uses. In this chapter we will be talking about Bible translations rather than marketing features.

Translation itself is unavoidable. God has revealed himself and has asked his people to make that communication known to others. Unless everyone wants to learn Hebrew and Greek (the Bible's original languages), we will need a translation. Translation is nothing more than transferring the message of one language into another language. We should not think of translation as a bad thing, since through translations we are able to hear what God has said. In other words, translations are necessary for people who speak a language other than Greek or Hebrew to understand what God is saying through his Word.

English Translations since 1611[9]

A number of more recent English translations have some connection (direct or indirect) to updating the King James Version. The *English Revised Version* (1881–1885) was the first such revision and the first English translation to make use of modern principles of textual criticism. As a result, the Greek text underlying the ERV was different from that of the KJV. In 1901 American scholars produced their own revision of the ERV: the *American Standard Version*. Toward the middle of the twentieth century (1946–1952), the *Revised Standard Version* appeared. The goal of the RSV translators was to capture the best of modern scholarship regarding the meaning of Scriptures and to express that meaning in English designed for public and private worship—the same qualities that had given the KJV such high standing in English literature.

The *New American Standard Bible* (1971, rev. ed. in 1995) claimed to be a revision of the ASV, but probably should be viewed as a new translation. The NASB (or NAS) is one of the more popular translations that adheres closely to the form of the original languages. The *New King James Version* (1979–1982) attempts to update the language of the KJV while retaining the same underlying Greek text that the translators of the KJV used (commonly called the *Textus Receptus* or TR).[10] This preference for the TR distinguishes the NKJV from the other revisions, which make use of a better Greek text (commonly called an *eclectic* Greek text), based on older and more reliable readings of the Greek.

The *New Revised Standard Version*, a thorough revision of the RSV, was completed in 1989 with the goal of being as literal as possible and as free as necessary. The accompanying chart illustrates the relationship between translations that are related in some way to revising the KJV.

In addition to the KJV revisions noted above, committees of scholars have produced many other new translations in recent years. Catholic scholars have completed two major translations: the *New American Bible* (1941–1970) and the *Jerusalem Bible* (1966). What makes these significant is that not until 1943 did the Roman Catholic Church permit scholars to translate from the original Greek and Hebrew. Until that time, their translation had to be based on the Latin Vulgate. The *New Jerusalem Bible*, a revision of the Jerusalem Bible, appeared in 1985.

Both the *New English Bible* (1961 – 1970) and its revision, the *Revised English Bible* (1989), are translations into contemporary British idiom. The American Bible Society completed the *Good News Bible* in 1976 (also called *Today's English*

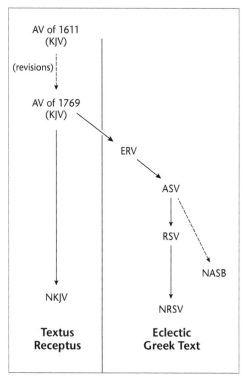

Version). The translators of this version sought to express the meaning of the original text in conversational English (even for those with English as a second language). In the *New International Version* (1973 – 1978), a large committee of evangelical scholars sought to produce a translation in international English, offering a middle ground between a word-for-word approach and a thought-for-thought approach.

The *New Century Version* (1987) and the *Contemporary English Version* (1991 – 1995) are recent translations that utilize a simplified, thought-for-thought approach to translation. A similar translation from the translators of the NIV is the *New International Reader's Version* (1995 – 1996).

The *New Living Translation* (1996) is a fresh, thought-for-thought translation based on the popular paraphrase, the *Living Bible* (1967 – 1971). A recent attempt by an individual (rather than a committee) to render the message of Scripture in the language of today's generation is *The Message* by Eugene Peterson (1993–2002). *The Message* claims to be a translation but reads more like a paraphrase aimed at grabbing the reader's attention. *Today's New International Version* (2001) is a revision of the NIV, using the best of contemporary biblical scholarship and changes in the English language.

The *English Standard Version* (2001) is a word-for-word translation that uses the RSV as its starting point. Its goal is to be as literal as possible while maintaining beauty, dignity of expression, and literary excellence. The *Holman Christian Standard Bible* (1999–2004) is a new Bible translation that promotes a word-for-word approach unless clarity and readability demand a more idiomatic translation, in which case the literal form is often put in a footnote.

The *New English Translation*, commonly referred to as the NET Bible (1998), offers an electronic version of a modern translation for distribution over the Internet. Anyone anywhere in the world with an Internet connection (including translators and missionaries) can have access to this new version (and its more than 60,000 translation notes), not to mention that it is under continual revision.

Now let's explore the different approaches translators take when making a translation.

Approaches to Translating God's Word

The process of translating is more complicated than it appears. Some people think that all you have to do when making a translation is to define each word and string together all the individual word meanings. This assumes that the source language (in this case, Greek or Hebrew) and the receptor language (such as English) are exactly alike. If life could only be so easy! In fact, no two languages are exactly alike. For example, look at a verse chosen at random—from the story of Jesus healing a demon-possessed boy (Matthew 17:18). The word-for-word English rendition is written below a transliteration of the Greek:

> *Kai epetimēsen autō ho Iēsous kai exēlthen ap' autou to daimonion*
> And rebuked it the Jesus and came out from him the demon

kai etherapeuthē ho pais apo tēs hōras ekeinēs
and was healed the boy from the hour   that

Should we conclude that the English line presented above is the most accurate translation of Matthew 17:18 because it attempts a literal rendering of the verse? Is a translation better if it tries to match each word in the source language with a corresponding word in a receptor language? Could you even read an entire Bible "translated" in this way?

The fact that no two languages are exactly alike makes translation a complicated endeavor. D. A. Carson identifies a number of things that separate one language from another:[11]

- No two words are exactly alike. Words mean different things in different languages. Even words that are similar in meaning differ in some way. For example, the Greek verb *phileō*, often translated "to love," must be translated "to kiss" when Judas kisses Jesus in an act of betrayal (Matthew 26:48 in both KJV and NIV).
- The vocabulary of any two languages will vary in size. This means that it is impossible to assign a word in a source language directly to a word in a receptor language. This kind of one-to-one correspondence would be nice, but it is simply not possible.
- Languages put words together differently to form phrases, clauses, and sentences (syntax). This means that there are preset structural differences between any two languages. For example, English has an indefinite article ("a, an"), while Greek does not. In English adjectives come before the noun they modify and they use the same definite article (e.g., "the big city"). In Hebrew, however, adjectives come after the noun they modify and they have their own definite article (e.g., "the city, the big").
- Languages have different stylistic preferences. Sophisticated Greek emphasizes passive voice verbs, while refined English stresses the active voice. Hebrew poetry will sometimes use an acrostic pattern, which is impossible to transfer into English.

Since languages differ in many ways, making a translation is not a simple, cut-and-dried, mechanical process. When it comes to translation, it is wrong to assume that *literal* automatically equals *accurate*. A more literal translation is not necessarily a more accurate translation; it could actually be a less accurate translation. Is the translation "and was healed the boy from the hour that" better than "and the boy was cured at once" (NASB) or "and the child was healed from that moment" (NET Bible)? Translation is more than just finding matching words and adding them up.

Translation entails "reproducing the meaning of a text that is in one language (the *source language*), as fully as possible, in another language (the *receptor language*)."[12] The form of the original language is important and translators should stay with it when possible, but form should not have priority over meaning. What is most important is that the contemporary reader understands the meaning of the original text. When a translator can reproduce meaning while preserving form, all the better.

Translating is complicated work and translators often must make difficult choices between two equally good, but different ways of saying something. This explains why there are different approaches to translation. Individuals and committees have differences of opinion about the best way to make the tough choices involved in translation, including the relationship between form and meaning.

There are two main approaches to translation: the *formal* approach (sometimes labeled "literal" or "word-for-word") and the *functional* approach (often called "idiomatic" or "thought-for-thought"). In reality, no translation is entirely formal or entirely functional. Since source and receptor languages differ, all translations will have at least some formal features and some functional features. The situation is more like a scale, ranging from translations that are more formal to translations that are more functional (see below).

The *more formal* approach tries to stay as close as possible to the structure and words of the source language. Translators using this approach feel a keen responsibility to reproduce the forms of the original Greek and Hebrew whenever possible. The NASB, the ESV, and the HSCB use this approach. On the downside, the formal approach is less sensitive to the receptor language of the contemporary reader and, as a result, may appear stilted or awkward. Formal translations run the risk of sacrificing meaning for the sake of maintaining form.

The *more functional* approach tries to express the meaning of the original text in today's language. Here the translator feels a responsibility to reproduce the meaning of the original text in English so that the effect on today's reader is equivalent to the effect on the ancient reader.

Many contemporary translations utilize this approach, including the NIV, NLT, and GNB. The functional approach is not always as sensitive as it should be to the wording and structure of the source language. When it moves too far away from the form of the source language, the functional approach runs the risk of distorting the true meaning of the text. The spectrum of translations might look something like this, moving from the more formal to the more functional.

More Formal								More Functional	
KJV	NASB	RSV	NRSV	NAB	NIV	NJB	NCV	GNB	The Message
ASV	NKJV	HCSB	NET		TNIV	REB	NLT	CEV	
	ESV								

In addition to the two main approaches to translation discussed above, you will encounter what is known as a *paraphrase*. Technically, a paraphrase is not a translation from the original languages at all, but merely a restatement or explanation of a particular English translation using different English words. The *Living Bible* (1967 – 1971), perhaps the most famous paraphrase, is Kenneth Taylor's restatement of the *American Standard Version* (1901) for the benefit of his children.

Another translation similar to a paraphrase is the *Amplified Bible* (1958 – 1965), which tries to give the reader an understanding of the many meanings contained in a particular verse through the "creative use of amplification." For instance, John 11:25 reads: "Jesus said to her, I am [Myself] the Resurrection and the Life. Whoever believes in (adheres to, trusts in, and relies on) Me, although he may die, yet he shall live." Since any one word does not bring its full range of meaning into every context, the *Amplified Bible* leaves the misleading impression that the reader is free to choose from among the options presented.

Again, paraphrases are not translations from the original language. We do not recommend using paraphrases for serious study because they tend to explain rather than translate. We believe that the author's meaning is encoded in the details of the text. In a paraphrase the "translator" makes far too many of the interpretive decisions for you. The result is that paraphrases add many things that are simply not in the Bible. Rather than translating the Word of God, paraphrases present a commentary on the Word of God. You should treat paraphrases like commentaries and use them as such. Our advice for those who are addicted to the *Living Bible* and other paraphrases is to switch to the *New Living Translation*.

Choosing a Translation

We suggest the following guidelines for choosing a translation:

1. Choose a translation that uses modern English. The whole point of making a translation is to move the message of the original text to a language you can understand. History teaches us that languages change over time, and English is no exception. The English of John Wycliffe's day or of 1611 is simply not the same as the English of the twenty-first century. There is little to be gained by translating a Greek or Hebrew text into a kind of English that you no longer use and can no longer comprehend. For that reason, we recommend that you choose among the many good translations that have appeared within the last fifty years.

2. Choose a translation that is based on the standard Hebrew and Greek text. The standard text for the Old Testament is the *Biblia Hebraica Stuttgartensia (BHS)*. For the New Testament the standard text is reflected in the latest edition of the United Bible Societies' *Greek New Testament (GNT)* or Nestle-Aland's *Novum Testamentum Graece*. Along with the majority of scholars, we much prefer an eclectic text to the *Textus Receptus* used by the KJV and the NKJV.

3. Give preference to a translation by a committee over a translation by an individual. Translating requires an enormous amount of knowledge and skill. A group of qualified translators will certainly possess more expertise than any one translator possibly could. In addition, a group of scholars will usually guard against the tendency of individual scholars to read their own personal biases into their translation.

4. Choose a translation that is appropriate for your own particular purpose at the time. When you want to read devotionally or read to children, consider a simplified, functional translation such as the *New Living Translation* or the *New Century Version*. If you are reading to nontraditional or unchurched people, consider the *Contemporary English Version* or *The Message*. If you are reading to people with English as a second language, consider the *Good News Bible*. If you are reading to a "King-James-only" church, consider the *New King James*. But for your own personal serious Bible study, we suggest the *New American Standard Bible*, the *New International Version*, *Today's New International Version*, the *New Revised Standard Version*, the *English Standard Version*, the *Holman Christian Standard Bible*, or the *NET Bible*.

Conclusion

In this chapter we have learned about Bible translations. Few things are as important as how the Bible has been translated. We can be thankful that God has used translators to get the message of the original text into our hands. Can you imagine the Christian life without your own copy of God's Word? In spite of the many good Bible translations available to us, there is no such thing as a perfect translation. Furthermore, languages change over time. For these reasons, committed scholars and linguists must continue to work hard to get the message of the original text into a language that people can understand. Who knows, God may call you to serve as a Bible translator.

Discussion Questions

1. Which approach to Bible translation do you prefer? Why?
2. Why does "literal" not automatically equate to "accurate" when it comes to Bible translation?
3. Which particular translations do you like to compare as you study a passage of Scripture?

Writing Assignment

Select five translations that we talked about in this chapter. Select a passage from the Bible (it must be at least two verses long) and write out how the translations render this passage. Next, mark or highlight the differences among the five translations. Write a paragraph summarizing what you have observed by comparing the translations.

Meaning and Application

8

Who Controls the Meaning, the Reader or the Author?

When Danny's kids were small, one of their favorite videos was the old movie *The Wizard of Oz*. This movie is based on the book by L. Frank Baum. To Danny's young children this delightful tale was about a young girl named Dorothy and her cute dog, Toto, who overcame the odds and defeated the powerful and scary "bad guys" (the wicked witches) with some help from Dorothy's nice new friends. To the young children the story had this simple meaning.

If we observe the story closely, however, and if we start to poke around into the historical background of the time Baum wrote the book, a different meaning surfaces. One of the hottest political debates going on in America when Baum wrote this story was over the issue of whether America should continue to use the gold standard as the basis for the U.S. dollar or whether it should switch to silver. This historical context suggests that the main line of the book ("Follow the yellow brick road!") may be a reference to the central political issue of the day. Remember that although the yellow brick road led to the great wizard of Oz, once Dorothy arrived there, she discovered he was a fraud. Dorothy's real hope lay in her shoes. In Baum's book the shoes are *silver*. Hollywood changed them to ruby so they would show up better in color for the movie. So, perhaps the book falls into the classification of political satire.

According to this line of interpretation, the characters in the story then probably represent different segments of American society. The Scarecrow represents the farmers (supposedly, no brains). Who would the Tin Woodsman represent? The factory workers (no heart). And the cowardly lion perhaps represents the political leadership of the country.

85

We also meet the wicked witch of the east (the East Coast establishment?) and the wicked witch of the west (the West Coast establishment?). And who is the heroine? Middle America — Dorothy from Kansas.[13]

So, who is right? Are Danny's kids *wrong* to interpret the story as a simple tale of good triumphing over evil? Did not the author intend it to be read as political satire? Are we wrong if we understand it otherwise? What *is* the meaning of the story? And *who* determines that meaning?

This question about meaning has prompted a lively and sometimes heated debate, not only in secular literary circles, but also among students and scholars of the Bible. Throughout the first half of the twentieth century, the traditional approach to interpreting any literature, biblical or secular, was to assume that the author determines the meaning and the reader's job is to find that meaning. Within the world of secular literary criticism, however, this approach came under attack throughout the latter half of the twentieth century, and many literary critics today argue that it is the *reader*, and not the *author*, who determines what a text *means*.

This view has drifted over from secular literary criticism into the field of biblical interpretation. Many biblical scholars began probing the question, *What is meaning?* Some concluded that the term *meaning* only applies as a reader interacts with a text — that it takes both reader and text to produce *meaning*. The author, they argue, is no longer involved.

Of course, there remain those who maintain that the original author still controls the meaning. As an author writes, they argue, he or she intends to convey a certain meaning in the text. This intended meaning of the author's is the true meaning of the text.

The position that stresses the author in the determination of meaning is called *authorial intention*. The opposing view, which focuses on the reader as the main character in the determination of meaning, is called *reader response*. Both positions have strong arguments. Which approach should we take?

Communication — the Central Issue

Certainly the reader has the freedom to interpret a text any way he or she chooses. No one will force you to read *The Wonderful Wizard of Oz* as political satire. So the author has control of the meaning only so far as the reader allows him to. But suppose, for example, that you receive a mushy love poem written to you by your girlfriend or boyfriend. As you read each word and line of the poem, you will be searching for the meaning that your girlfriend or boyfriend intended. You will want to know what he or she is trying to say *to you.* In this situation you will be following the *authorial intention* approach because you are viewing the text as *communication* between the author and yourself. You know the author and you want to know what the author is saying to you. You will be asking the interpretive question, *What does the author mean?*

Let's assume, however, that one day as you walk through the woods, you find a piece of paper on the ground with a love poem written on it. The author is not even identified. The poem, however, is beautiful, and you enjoy it as you read. In this situation you may not care what the author intended or what the author meant. You do not even know who the author is. You have the freedom in this situation to read and interpret according to *reader response.* Your interpretive question will change to *What does this mean to me?* In the woods with an anonymous poem you are free to ignore the author and his or her meaning.

In many situations, however, it is extremely important that we search for the author's meaning because of serious negative consequences that will come if we misunderstand or intentionally ignore the meaning the author intended. For example, one of the most common literary texts in America is the big word STOP painted on the red octagonal signs at many street intersections across the country. If you choose to, you can follow a *reader response* approach and interpret the text to mean: *slow down just a bit, look for cars, and then speed on through the intersection.* Or perhaps it means Spin Tires On Pavement! The police, however, believe strongly in *authorial intent* for the determination of meaning, so they will respond to your interpretation with a traffic ticket and fine.

The issue of communication, therefore, lies at the heart of one's decision about how to interpret a text. If you, the reader, see the text as a communication between the author and yourself, you should search for the meaning that the *author intended.* If, however, you as the reader do not care to communicate with the author, then you are free to follow *reader response* and interpret the text without asking what the author meant. In some cases, however, there may be negative consequences for such a reading.

Can you see how this discussion applies to reading and interpreting the Bible? This is an important issue—one that lies at the foundation of our approach to interpreting Scripture. If you read the Bible merely as great literature, merely for its aesthetic value, or merely for its suggestive moral guidance, not as communication from God, then you can interpret the text in any way you choose. Your main interpretive question will be: *What does this text mean to me?* If, however, you believe that the Bible is God's revelatory Word to you and that the Scriptures function as communication from God to you, you should interpret the Bible by looking for the meaning that God, the author, intended. Your interpretive question should be: *What is the meaning God intended in this text?*

We believe strongly that the Bible is a revelation from God to us. God's purpose is to *communicate* with us about himself and his will for us. We can choose to ignore his message and interpret biblical texts according to our feelings and desires, but if we do, we will suffer the consequences of disobedience. We will also miss out on knowing God in the way he desires. So it is essential that we follow the *authorial intent* approach to interpreting the Bible. In biblical interpretation, the reader does not control the meaning; the author controls the meaning. This conclusion leads us to one of the most basic principles of our interpretive approach: *We do not create the meaning. Rather, we seek to discover the meaning that has been placed there by the author.*

Definitions

At this juncture it is also important that we define the terms *meaning* and *application*. We will use the term *meaning* to refer to that which the author wishes to convey with his signs.[14] Signs are simply the different conventions of written language—grammar, syntax, word meanings, and so on. Thus, in biblical interpretation meaning is not determined by the reader. Meaning is what the author intended to communicate when he wrote the text.

What the reader does with the meaning is *application*. Once we identify the meaning in the text that God is trying to communicate to us, then we must respond to that meaning. We use the term *application* to refer to the response of the reader to the meaning of the text. Thus, it would be incorrect for us to ask in a Bible study, "What does this passage *mean* to you?" The correct question sequence is, "What does this passage *mean*? How should you *apply* this meaning to your life?"

Applying the Meaning

We cannot apply the Bible without knowing what it means, but we can know the Bible without applying it. We can investigate context, analyze words, and even memorize chapters, but unless we act on what we know, we do not truly understand that Word. Knowledge by itself is not enough; it should lead to action.

We began the Interpretive Journey by discovering the meaning of the text in the town of the biblical audience. Then we measured the width of the river of differences and crossed the principlizing bridge. Now it is time to ask, "How can we apply the meaning of the text in our town?"

Keep in mind that there is a vast difference between knowing how to apply a biblical text and actually applying that text in your life. Once you know how a text could be applied, it is up to you to submit to the Spirit of God and live out the application. For example, in Ephesians 4:26 we are told not to let the sun go down while we are still angry. We find in this verse the *theological principle* of putting a fairly short time limit on dealing with anger. As a volatile emotion, if anger goes unchecked for long, it can do major damage. One *application* of this principle would be to make sure that when you get angry with your spouse or someone at work, you deal with the problem as soon as possible (e.g., before the end of the day).

We will now show you how to determine valid applications for theological principles you have discovered in a biblical text. Since applications may vary from reader to reader, we need a reliable method of making sure that the applications are within the boundaries established by the author's meaning. Our approach to applying biblical meaning follows the steps of the Interpretive Journey you are already familiar with (see chapter 1). We can expand Step 4 as we detail the application process into several substeps:

a. Observe how the principles in the text address the original situation.
b. Discover a parallel situation in a contemporary context.
c. Make your application specific.

We will illustrate the application of process using Philippians 4:13, a popular text that is often misapplied: "I can do everything through him [Christ] who gives me strength." In each section, we will cite the step, discuss the process, and then apply it to our example.

Step 1: Grasp the text in their town by summarizing the original situation (historical-cultural context) and the meaning of the text for the biblical audience.

Regarding Philippians 4:13, we should note that Paul is writing this letter while in prison awaiting trial (1:7, 13–14, 17). His faithfulness to Christ in the ministry of the gospel has landed him in prison. In this friendship letter, he exhorts the Philippians to stand firm in the face of external opposition and warns them against internal fighting. He reports about his own situation and thanks them for their ministry to him. In Philippians 4:10–13, Paul acknowledges their monetary gift sent through their mutual friend, Epaphroditus. He also wants to make it clear that while he is most grateful for their gift, his ministry is ultimately dependent on Christ.

Step 2: Measure the width of the river to cross. What are the differences between the biblical situation and our situation?

When we interpret New Testament letters, normally the river is not very wide or deep. There are exceptions, of course (e.g., dealing with the passage about meat offered to idols in 1 Corinthians), but usually this is the case. Regarding the Philippians passage, there are a few differences. Paul is an apostle and we are not apostles. Paul is in prison and most of us have not been imprisoned for our faith (or for any other reason, we hope). Neither are we members of the Philippian church that have supported Paul's ministry financially.

But there are also similarities. We are New Testament Christians under the same covenant. We are also members of Christ's body, the church.

Moreover, many of us experience difficult situations as we seek to live out our faith. For the most part, the river of differences for Philippians 4:13 is not wide.

Step 3: Cross the principlizing bridge. List the theological principles communicated by the passage.

As for Philippians 4:13, you could say, "Believers can learn to be content in a variety of circumstances through Christ, who gives them strength." Or you might prefer, "Christ will give believers strength to be content in a variety of trying circumstances that come as a result of following him faithfully."

Step 4: Grasp the text in our town. How should individual Christians today apply the theological principles in their lives? This step consists of several substeps.

a. Observe how the principles in the text address the original situation.

Look carefully at how the biblical principle addresses the historical-cultural situation. What you see in this intersection between the text and the situation is the heart and soul of the application process. There will be certain *key elements* present in the intersection of text and situation that will prove significant for the rest of the application process.

As the principle in Philippians 4:13 intersects with the historical-cultural situation, several key elements emerge:

Element 1:	A Christian (Paul)
Element 2:	A Christian who is experiencing a variety of trying circumstances as a result of following Christ faithfully (Paul is in prison because of his service in the cause of Christ)
Element 3:	Christ's promise to give the Christian strength to endure whatever the circumstances

With key elements in hand we are ready to connect to our world and make application to our lives.

b. Discover a parallel situation in a contemporary context.

In applying the Bible we have to be students not only of the biblical world but also of our own world. Search for a situation in your life (or your world) that parallels the biblical situation. When we speak of a *parallel* situation, we mean a situation that contains *all* of the key elements you identified in the previous step.

Below we provide two scenarios. The first is only an apparent parallel situation since it does not contain all the key elements; the second is a genuine parallel that does contain all the key elements.

Example 1. Philippians 4:13 has become a popular theme verse for Christian athletes in American society. The verse was even prominently displayed on the robe of a recent championship boxer. The phrase "I can do everything" no doubt motivated the boxer to defeat his opponent or at least to do his best.

Assuming that Paul and the boxer are both Christians (element 1 above) and that they both look to Christ for strength (element 3), we are still missing at least one key element of the intersection between the original situation and the text (element 2). Paul and the boxer have radically different understandings of the expression, "I can do everything." A close look at the literary context of Philippians 4:13 reveals that the word "everything" refers to a variety of trying circumstances. At this point in his life, Paul is experiencing a trial of need rather than a trial of plenty. When Paul says he can "do everything," he is referring to being content or enduring rather than conquering. There is a big difference between the "trials" of athletic competition and the trial of being imprisoned for your faith.

We misapply the Bible when we grab a situation that is not a genuine parallel. There may be a superficial connection, but one or more of the key elements are missing. Ultimately when we misapply the Bible, we hurt people by pointing them toward false realities. People put their hope in something they think is true when it is not, and they suffer for it. In our example from Philippians, the principle of contentment in Christ whatever the circumstances is replaced by a proof text calling on God to help us win the game or the contest. How does this misapplication affect the faith of a losing boxer? Couldn't the boxer actually apply this verse more appropriately after a serious defeat? What do you suppose God should do if this boxer fought another Christian boxer who also claimed the promise of Philippians 4:13?

Example 2. You are a single mother whose non-Christian husband recently deserted you because of your commitment to Christ. Your two small children suddenly find themselves without a father. The sense of personal failure weighs heavy. The social pressure of what people will say lingers. You face overwhelming financial burdens and worry about how you will survive on your part-time job. As life seems to crumble around you, God has given you an unshakable peace that Jesus Christ is with you, that he understands, and that he will see you through.

In this last scenario all the key elements are present: (1) a Christian (2) who is experiencing tough circumstances because of his or her commitment to Christ (3) but who looks to Christ for strength to endure. As you identify contemporary situations that are parallel, you can have confidence that you are applying the meaning of the biblical text rather than an invented meaning. The next step is to be even more specific with your application.

c. Make your applications specific.

Once you have identified a parallel situation — a genuine parallel — you should give some thought to specific ways the biblical principle(s) might apply. What should the single mother think or do as she turns to Christ for strength? (We say *think* or *do* because applications may touch on ways of thinking as well as ways of acting or behaving.) If we never make our applications specific, people may not know how to live out the message of the Bible in the down and dirty of real life. Don't be afraid to make specific suggestions. People don't just need to know *what* to do; they also need to know *how* to do it.

Perhaps the best way to make your applications specific is by creating *real-world scenarios*. These scenarios function as illustrations or examples of how a person might put the biblical principles into practice. They help us move beyond abstract principles to capture the color and emotion of the biblical principle. We are quick to admit that these real-world scenarios are not on the same level as inspired Scripture; they are merely illustrations. But we intend for them to be guided by the Holy Spirit and to be faithful to the biblical principles (i.e., consistent with the author's intended meaning). We also want the contemporary audience to know that God's Word is eternally relevant. Real-world scenarios should be both faithful to the meaning of the text and relevant to the contemporary audience. Let's give it a try.

Example. A real-world scenario making specific applications for the single mother as introduced above.

As a single mother you could do several things — get counsel from a mature Christian, write down your thoughts, and pray honestly. You may also want to study other biblical passages that speak about husband – wife relations, divorce, remarriage, and so forth. God will give you wisdom as you search his Word. There may be business people in your church who could assist you in making financial plans. Having a plan to provide for your kids will ease many of the day-to-day worries.

What about your husband? Throughout this entire ordeal you have been a faithful wife. You have prayed constantly that your husband would allow the Lord to calm his restless spirit, but he made a decision to leave. He knew that your ultimate loyalty was to the Lord and that you would follow Christ above all, even him. While his leaving has been tougher than you ever imagined, you have come to know God's grace and peace in ways that are beyond explanation. While you are frightened about the prospects of going it alone, you are not really alone. Of this one thing you are now sure: Your Lord will never abandon you — never! He always keeps his promises. You can do all things through Christ.

Real-world scenarios furnish a wonderful way of making specific applications that are both faithful to the original meaning of the text and relevant to contemporary life. This approach works especially well when interpreting biblical stories since you don't have to create entirely new scenarios. Instead, you just retell the biblical story for the contemporary audience (an approach sometimes referred to as *contemporization*). To contemporize a biblical story you retell the story so that the effect on the contemporary audience is equivalent to the effect on the original audience. We translate the meaning of the story into our own context and reproduce its effects on the contemporary audience.

One word of caution is in order concerning real-world scenarios. You need to study the biblical passage carefully, especially the historical-cultural and literary contexts, so that the real-world scenario you develop will accurately reflect the meaning of the biblical text. Otherwise you will be making a specific application for a biblical text that doesn't exist. It takes discipline, hard work, and creativity to come up with a scenario or to retell a story in a way that is both relevant to the contemporary audience and faithful to the original meaning. Please, please do your homework so that your scenario will reflect that meaning.

Conclusion

Our approach to interpreting the Bible focuses on *authorial intent* rather than *reader response*. God has communicated with us through the Scriptures. He has worked through human authors to convey his meaning to us through the text. As readers we do not create the meaning; rather, we seek to find the meaning that has already been placed into the text by the author (both divine and human). This is why an understanding of careful reading, historical background, literary context, and translations is so important. These are the items we must grapple with if we are to determine the intended meaning of God, the author.

This also completes our approach to applying the meaning of the Bible. Because God's character and human nature do not change, his Word remains relevant! Our principlizing approach gives you a way to journey into God's Word that is relevant for every generation — not only for us, but also for our children, our grandchildren, our great grandchildren, and so on.

Some of you might be concerned that this method will restrict your freedom to apply the Scriptures. We remind you that as faithful readers our job is not to invent new meaning, but to apply the meaning that has been inscribed in the biblical text. Don't worry. You'll be able to find a number of parallel situations in your life or in your world that do contain all the key elements. And when you find a genuine parallel, you can be confident that you are applying the real meaning of the biblical text. Also, don't be afraid to make your applications specific by creating real-world scenarios or by contemporizing a biblical story. People need illustrations and examples of how the meaning might be lived out in real life. God wants his Word to sink deep into our hearts and minds and transform the way we live.

Before we move into the next chapters where you will learn how to interpret the various literary types found in the New Testament, we need to remember the main reason we come to the Bible in the first place. We study Scripture not just to learn more *about God*, but to *know and love God more.* He gave us his Word not just to fill our brains with biblical facts, but to change our lives. The plain intention of the divine Author is that we would understand God's Word and then apply it. Or, as Jesus said in John 14:21: "Whoever has my commands and obeys them, he is the one who loves me."

Discussion Questions

1. Why is the issue of who determines meaning (the author or the reader) such an important issue when it comes to studying the Bible?
2. Why is the issue of communication important to the discussion of authorial intent?
3. In the application process, why it is crucial to observe *all* the key elements that emerge from the intersection of the theological principle of the passage and the original situation?

Writing Assignment

Read Jesus' parable of the good Samaritan in Luke 10:30–35. Contemporize the parable by writing a story of your own that retells the original story so that the effect on the contemporary audience is equivalent to the effect on the original audience.

9

*B*uried in the top of a closet in the Duvall house are two shoeboxes filled with "mushies." For two years before Scott and Judy were married, they lived three hundred miles apart and survived by making frequent phone calls, taking occasional trips, and writing lots of letters. The two shoeboxes are packed with love letters. Some are short, others long; some informative, others playful; some serious, others silly; but all are valuable pieces of communication between two people who loved (and continue to love) each other very much.

Letters play an important role in our lives. How do you feel when you get a personal note in the mail? Do you remember the letter informing you of your acceptance into a particular school? What about the long letter of advice from a parent or trusted friend? Have you ever received a "Dear John" letter or a DTR ("define-the-relationship") letter? Have you ever written one? Then there are business letters, legal letters, medical letters, personal letters, and so on. Whether by email, by text-message, on official letterhead, on personal stationery, or on the back of a napkin, we write notes and letters to communicate what we think and how we feel.

Of course, letters predate the Duvall romance. They were used widely in the ancient world and figure prominently in our New Testament. Twenty-one of the twenty-seven books of the New Testament are letters (about 35 percent of the entire New Testament).[15] Most evangelical scholars agree that Paul, James, Peter, John, Jude, and the author of Hebrews (who chose to write anonymously) are responsible for those twenty-one letters.

Paul	?	James	Peter	John	Jude
Romans	Hebrews	James	1 Peter	1 John	Jude
1 Corinthians			2 Peter	2 John	
2 Corinthians				3 John	
Galatians					
Ephesians					
Philippians					
Colossians					
1 Thessalonians					
2 Thessalonians					
1 Timothy					
2 Timothy					
Titus					
Philemon					

Characteristics of New Testament Letters

New Testament letters are *typically longer* than their ancient counterparts since early Christian leaders needed more space to conduct their missionary work and shepherd their flocks from a distance. They needed extra room to say hello and goodbye, bring their readers up to date, encourage and instruct, tackle difficult issues, warn against false teaching, and much more. Also, some New Testament letters are more formal (e.g., Romans, Ephesians, Hebrews, James, and 1 Peter) while others are less formal (e.g., Philemon, 2 John, and 3 John).

The letters of our New Testament were considered *authoritative substitutes* for the personal presence of men like Paul, Peter, and John. When these apostles and other leaders were unable to address a problem or deal with a situation in person, they did the next best thing: They wrote a letter. The letter provided a way for early Christian leaders to express their views and minister from a distance. These letters were authoritative substitutes for the leaders themselves (e.g., Gal. 1:1; Eph. 1:1; 2 Peter 1:1). Their letters of instruction, warning, and encouragement carry authority because they write as Christ's authentic representatives.

New Testament letters are *occasional* or *situational*, meaning that they were written to address specific situations or problems related to the author or (usually) to the readers. Those who wrote New Testament letters did so in order to meet the practical needs of those receiving the letters (e.g., to clarify an issue, address a doctrinal problem, or confront readers about their behavior). As a result, when interpreting New Testament letters we must be careful not to conclude too much from only one letter and we should do our best to reconstruct the situation that called for the letter in the first place.

New Testament letters were *carefully written and delivered*. The actual job of writing down a letter was normally assigned to a trained scribe or secretary (*amanuensis*). In Romans 16:22, the secretary even identifies himself: "I, Tertius, who wrote down this letter, greet you in the Lord." This does not mean that Tertius was the author of Romans, but he served as Paul's secretary in this instance. Also, New Testament letters often included cosenders (e.g., Timothy, Silas, Sosthenes) who were significantly involved in ministry among the people to whom the letters were addressed.

After a finished copy of the letter had been prepared, it was delivered. Average citizens depended largely on people who happened to be traveling in the direction that the letter needed to go. Paul used trusted friends such as Tychicus to carry his letters (e.g., Eph. 6:21–22; Col. 4:7–9). Letters were expensive endeavors and faithful carriers were important, not only to deliver the letter safely but also to elaborate on the details of the letter in person.

New Testament letters were *intended for use in the Christian community*. They were meant to be read aloud again and again to specific congregations. We normally read the Bible silently to ourselves. But for a variety of reasons, people in the first century preferred to hear their letters read aloud. For one thing, letters were too valuable to loan out to families or individuals. Also, Jewish Christians were accustomed to hearing the Scriptures read aloud in services of worship from their days in the synagogue. And, of course, some Christians simply could not read.

Consequently, letters were normally presented orally for the benefit of the group. We get a glimpse of this in the book of Revelation, where a blessing is pronounced on the person who reads (aloud) the words of the prophecy to the listening congregation (see Revelation 1:3).

How to Interpret New Testament Letters

To interpret a New Testament letter, we return to the four steps of the Interpretive Journey discussed in chapter 1.

Step 1: Grasp the text in their town. What did the text mean to the biblical audience?

You need to get a feel for the whole letter, and the best way to do this is by reading the letter in one sitting. Both ancient and contemporary letters were meant to be read from start to finish. Don't let the chapter-and-verse divisions in your Bible tempt you to skip around and read only small sections of the letter in isolation.

Since letters are occasional or situational, the next step in discovering what the text meant to the biblical audience is to reconstruct the historical-cultural context of the biblical writer and his audience. Use a good study Bible, along with Bible dictionaries and commentaries, to find out about the author, the audience, and their circumstances, along with the purpose of the letter. Summarize your reconstruction of the situation in a paragraph or two.

After you have an idea about the situation of the author and the recipients, you need to identify the literary context of the specific passage you are studying. In the case of New Testament letters, remember to *think paragraphs!*[16] Summarize the main point of the paragraph that comes before your passage, the one that contains your passage, and the one that comes right after your passage. Find out how these paragraphs link together to communicate the author's message. Use your observation skills to read the text carefully (remember what you learned in chapters 2 and 3). Look for details. Notice important connections. Finally, write out a statement of what the passage meant to the first-century audience.

Step 2: Measure the width of the river to cross. What are the differences between the biblical audience and us?

In New Testament letters, the river of differences is not usually wide. Nevertheless, even in these letters the river can sometimes present a challenge. Although they were written to Christians like us, they sometimes dealt with situations foreign to us. After examining your passage, write a paragraph describing the differences that define the width of the river you need to cross.

Step 3: Cross the principlizing bridge. What theological principles are in this text?

Here we are looking for theological principles reflected in the meaning of the text you identified in Step 1. God not only gives specific expressions of meaning to biblical audiences, he also sends a broader, theological message through these same texts to all of his people. In light of how our situation compares to and differs from the situation of the biblical audience, try to identify the theological principles reflected in the text. Write out the principle (or principles) in a sentence or two, using present-tense verbs.

In his book *Applying the Bible*, Jack Kuhatschek mentions three questions that can help us locate theological principles in a passage.[17] (1) Does the author state a principle? Often in New Testament letters the author will state his message in the form of a theological principle (e.g., Eph. 6:1: "Children, obey your parents in the Lord").

(2) Does the broader context reveal a theological principle? Sometimes the author will supply a theological principle in the surrounding context. For example, in Ephesians 5:21 Paul writes, "Submit to one another out of reverence for Christ." He follows this general principle with specific examples of how people in the ancient household should submit to each other (wives/husbands, children/fathers, slaves/masters).

(3) We should ask why a particular command or instruction was given. Sometimes when you locate the reason behind the command or instruction, you will also find the theological principle. In Galatians 5:2 Paul writes, "I, Paul, tell you that if you let yourselves be circumcised, Christ will be of no value to you at all." When we ask why the apostle warns the Galatians against circumcision, we find the theological principle that people cannot achieve God's acceptance by keeping the law or by human effort alone (symbolized by circumcision). God's grace is given as a gift.

After you have written out your principle or principles in one or two sentences using present-tense verbs, ask the following questions to determine whether you have truly discovered a theological principle:

- Is the principle reflected in the biblical text?
- Is the principle timeless rather than tied to a specific situation?
- Is the principle culturally bound?[18]
- Is the principle consistent with the teaching of the rest of Scripture?
- Is the principle relevant to both the biblical and the contemporary audience?

Theological principles provide a bridge across the river of historical and cultural differences that separate the ancient text and the contemporary audience.

Step 4: Grasp the text in our town. How should individual Christians today apply the theological principles in their lives?

In the last phase of interpreting a New Testament letter, we apply the theological principle or principles to Christians today. Remember that while these principles are determined by the meaning of the text, they may be applied in a number of different ways today. There are three steps.

(1) We observe how the theological principles in the biblical text address the original situation. We identify the key elements that are present in the intersection between the principle and the situation.

(2) We search for a situation in our lives or our world that contains all the key elements. When we find such parallel contemporary situations, we can be confident that we are applying the meaning of the biblical text.

(3) We need to make our applications specific by creating real-world scenarios that are both faithful to the meaning of the text and relevant to the contemporary audience. Remember, in order to truly journey into God's Word, we need to obey what we learn.

Conclusion

Life would not be the same without letters. We use them to communicate our deepest thoughts and feelings, some of which can be quite "mushy." When we turn to the twenty-one letters of the New Testament, we catch a glimpse of the practical, frontline work of early Christian disciple-makers. These letters served as authoritative substitutes for leaders who could not always minister in person. They were written to address specific situations and meet the practical needs of their readers.

When you approach a New Testament letter, remember that it is a letter and not a telephone book. Letters are meant to be read from beginning to end, the same way you read a personal letter today. Take the historical-cultural situation seriously and place a high priority on tracing the author's flow of thought (i.e., the literary context). Then use the principlizing bridge to cross the river of differences and apply the meaning of the biblical text to your life.

The letters of the New Testament offer a window into the struggles and victories of the early church. They provide inspired instruction and advice for living a godly life, for which we can be forever grateful. We close this chapter with a typical closing from a New Testament letter: "Grace be with you. Amen."

Discussion Questions

1. How does knowing the situational nature of New Testament letters help you avoid misinterpretation?
2. Can you think of an example where chapter or verse divisions have actually led to common misinterpretation of Scripture?
3. Determining whether you have truly discovered a theological principle is an extremely significant step. What is the difference between a theological principle and a practical application?

Writing Assignment

Take one of the following passages through all four steps of the Interpretive Journey explained and illustrated in this chapter:

- Romans 8:26–27
- 1 Corinthians 11:27–32
- Galatians 5:16–18
- Colossians 3:1–4
- 2 Timothy 3:16–17
- Hebrews 4:12–13
- 1 Peter 5:6–7

New Testament — Gospels

10

At the very center of our faith stands a person — Jesus Christ. He performed miracles and spoke the very "words of eternal life" (John 6:68). But one thing Jesus never did was publish his own autobiography. Without a book from Jesus himself, how do we know anything about him?

Our most direct witness to Jesus comes from the four canonical Gospels: Matthew, Mark, Luke, and John. These four books comprise almost half of the New Testament in terms of percentage. In them the first followers of Jesus give us something similar to a biography of Jesus. The four Gospels are significant because they tell us the story of Jesus, the unique Son of God.

We begin this chapter by answering the question, "What are the Gospels?" in order to know how to read the Gospels as intended. Once we understand the nature of the Gospels, we can learn more about how to actually interpret them.

What Are the Gospels?

The term *gospel* translates the Greek word *euangelion*, which means "good news." First and foremost the Gospels are stories. They are powerful, interesting, and important stories of Jesus. But as stories, the Gospels are not exactly like modern biographies (e.g., they do not cover the entire life of Jesus, but jump from his birth to his public ministry). Often the Gospel writers arrange Jesus' actions topically rather than chronologically and report what Jesus says in a variety of ways.

Yet just because the Gospels differ from modern biographies does not mean they are not biographies; it simply means they are not *modern* biographies. Ancient biographers followed a different set of rules. Ancient biographies normally had a simple outline, beginning with the birth or arrival of the main character and ending with his death. The material between the main character's birth and death included stories and sayings selected and arranged by the author to tell the audience something important about the character.

If you have spent any time reading the Gospels, you will notice that while all four tell essentially the same story, the details vary from one Gospel to another. We really have four different versions of the one story of Jesus. For those of us who seem fixated on chronological strictness, the variety can cause problems. For example, how do we understand Matthew and Luke switching the order of the second and third temptations of Jesus (cf. Matt. 4:5–10 with Luke 4:5–13)?

On a larger scale, you will sometimes find considerable variation in the order of the same events as presented in the first three Gospels. Matthew, Mark, and Luke are commonly called the *Synoptic Gospels* since they can easily be "seen together" when placed side by side (*syn* means *together*; *optic* means *see*). John often takes a different course altogether. In the chart (on p.107) you can see how the first three Gospel writers place the same events and stories in slightly different order in their respective Gospels.[19]

We should begin by recognizing that the Gospel writers (like any reporter or historian) could not tell all that there was to tell about Jesus. John admits as much in the final sentence of his Gospel (21:25): "Jesus did many other things as well. If every one of them were written down, I suppose that even the whole world would not have room for the books that would be written." There was simply not enough time and not enough scroll space to tell the whole story. As a result, under the direction of the Spirit, the Gospel writers chose what to include and what to omit, as well as how to arrange the material in a way that effectively communicated the good news to their contemporaries.

Event	Matthew	Mark	Luke
Cleansing of leper	8:1 – 4	1:40 – 45	5:12 – 16
Centurion of Capernaum	8:5 – 13	no parallel	7:1 – 10
Peter's mother-in-law	8:14 – 15	1:29 – 31	4:38 – 39
Sick healed	8:16 – 17	1:32 – 34	4:40 – 41
Following Jesus	8:18 – 22	no parallel	9:57 – 62
Stilling the storm	8:23 – 27	4:35 – 41	8:22 – 25
Gadarene demoniac	8:28 – 34	5:1 – 20	8:26 – 39
Healing of the paralytic	9:1 – 8	2:1 – 12	5:17 – 26
Matthew's call	9:9 – 13	2:13 – 17	5:27 – 32
Fasting question	9:14 – 17	2:18 – 22	5:33 – 39
Jairus and the woman	9:18 – 26	5:21 – 43	8:40 – 56

As ancient biographers, the Gospel writers felt free to paraphrase or summarize what Jesus said and to arrange the events according to a particular theme rather than according to strict chronological sequence. In his prologue (Luke 1:1 – 4), Luke admits his use of eyewitness testimony and careful research in retelling the story of Jesus.

The goal of each Gospel writer was to tell the story of Jesus in a faithful, yet relevant and persuasive manner for their readers. Rather than viewing the differences between accounts as errors in reporting, we should see them as illustrations of the different theological purposes and emphases of the Gospel writers. Once we realize that the Gospel writers were operating under ancient rather than modern literary rules, many of the so-called discrepancies between the Gospels fade away.

Where does all of this lead us? We need to grasp the genre of gospel in order to read the Gospels properly. The four Gospels are similar in many ways to ancient biography, but they are more than ancient biography. By focusing on Jesus' life and teachings we may describe the Gospels accurately as *Christ-centered biography.* They are telling the story in order to teach their readers something about the person and mission of Jesus. The Gospel writers selected and arranged their material about Christ in order to communicate theological truth to their audience. All storytelling is storytelling for a particular purpose, and the purpose of Matthew, Mark, Luke, and John is thoroughly Christ-centered!

This brings us to the two primary purposes that the writers had in mind when writing their Gospels. (1) They have selected and arranged material to tell the story of Jesus. (2) Through the story of Jesus, they are saying something important to their first readers (and to us). Since the Holy Spirit saw fit to inspire the Gospels in this way, we need to adopt a way of reading them that matches the method used by the Gospel writers.

How Should We Read the Gospels?

Our method of reading the Gospels must respect the means God used to inspire them in the first place. The Gospel writers are saying something about Jesus *in* each episode and they are saying something *by the way* they link the smaller stories together to form the larger story.

To arrive at a method of reading the Gospels that matches the means of God's communication, let's transform these two central purposes cited above into two simple interpretive questions. (1) What does this small story tell us about Jesus? (2) What is the Gospel writer trying to say to his readers by the way that he puts the smaller stories together? The chart below depicts the two central interpretive questions for reading the Gospels.

Episode 1	Episode 2	Episode 3
What is this central message of this episode?	What is this central message of this episode?	What is this central message of this episode?
Episodes 1, 2, and 3		
What is the Gospel writer trying to communicate to his readers by the way he connects these stories together?		

Take the familiar story of Mary and Martha in Luke 10:38–42 as an example. Step 1 is to read each episode and understand its main message (see below).

Luke 10:25 – 37	Luke 10:38 – 42	Luke 11:1 – 13
We see that love for one's neighbor should transcend all human boundaries such as nationality, race, religion, or economic status.	Here we discover that doing good things for God can sometimes cause us to miss God himself. Martha's desire to put on a feast for Jesus causes her to miss the best thing: listening to Jesus.	Jesus teaches us how to communicate with God through prayer (11:1 – 4). This is followed by a parable on prayer (11:5 – 8) and an exhortation to pray (11:9 – 13).

In Step 2 we need to put the episode of Mary and Martha in Luke 10:38 – 42 alongside the surrounding episodes to see what Luke is trying to communicate by the way he has put the smaller stories together. Look at our summaries above and think about what these three stories have in common. Do you see any connections? Here is what we came up with.

Luke 10:25 – 37; 10:38 – 42; 11:1 – 13
The common theme seems to be relationships. In the first story we are told that followers of Jesus should be loving neighbors to people in need. In our second story we are taught that listening to Jesus should take priority over "religious activity." Finally Luke emphasizes our relationship to God in 11:1 – 13. Followers of Jesus need to know how to relate to their neighbors (service), how to relate to the Lord Jesus (devotion), and how to relate to their Father (prayer).

Special Literary Forms in the Gospels

As a teacher Jesus would never have been accused of being boring. One reason he was such an engaging teacher was that he conveyed his message through a wide array of literary forms and techniques.[20] We cannot discuss them all, but we want to give you some guidelines for understanding Jesus' use of exaggeration, metaphor and simile, irony, rhetorical questions, and parables.

Exaggeration

As a master teacher Jesus commonly used exaggeration (also called hyperbole) to connect in a powerful way with his listeners and drive home his point. Exaggeration occurs when a truth is overstated for the sake of effect to such an extent that a literal fulfillment is either impossible or completely ridiculous. Statements like "I studied forever for that test" or "I'm so hungry I could eat a horse" are examples of exaggeration. Here are two examples from the Gospels.

> If your right eye causes you to sin, gouge it out and throw it away.... If your right hand causes you to sin, cut if off and throw it away. It is better for you to lose one part of your body than for your whole body to go into hell. (Matt. 5:29–30)

> Children, how hard it is to enter the kingdom of God. It is easier for a camel to go through the eye of a needle than for a rich man to enter the kingdom of God. (Mark 10:24b–25)

When you see exaggeration in the Gospels, do not force a literal interpretation or you will miss the real meaning of the passage. We should take Scripture seriously but not always literally. Figurative language can carry a meaning (and corresponding application) every bit as radical as anything literal.

When you encounter exaggeration, ask the simple question: "What's the real point here?" In Matthew 5:29–30 Jesus is telling his followers to take drastic steps to avoid sexual sin. In Mark 10:24b–25 Jesus uses exaggeration to point out how difficult it will be for people who are focused on earthly wealth to enter the kingdom of God—more difficult, we might say, than squeezing a school bus through a keyhole.

Metaphor and Simile

When Jesus says to his disciples, "You are the salt of the earth" (Matt. 5:13), or to the teachers of the law and the Pharisees, "You are like whitewashed tombs" (Matt. 23:27), he is using metaphor and simile, respectively. Both literary vehicles make comparisons. When interpreting metaphors and similes, locate the intended point of the comparison. Disciples are compared to salt in order to underscore their responsibility to permeate and stop the decay in society. Teachers of the law and Pharisees are compared to whitewashed tombs in the sense that their outward appearance covers up spiritual decay going on underneath.

You get the idea. Find the comparison intended by the author and you have found the meaning of the metaphor or simile.

Narrative Irony

Irony is grounded in the principle of contrast — contrast between what is expected and what actually happens. You might say that there is an unexpected twist to the story. Someone hearing the story of Mary and Martha for the first time might expect Jesus to tell Mary to get up and help her sister, but, as you know, that is not how things turn out. When the dust settles in Mark 4–5, the uncontrollable, demon-possessed man has been restored to his right mind, while the demon-possessed pigs (an appalling combination especially for Jews) return to the sea, the same sea that produced the storm the disciples had just been through.

The primary interpretive goal is to notice irony in the first place. After you detect irony, take time to reflect on the unexpected turn of events. What contrasts are present? What if things had actually turned out as expected? What does the twist in the story reveal about our own expectations?

Rhetorical Questions

Jesus is fond of rhetorical questions, questions designed to make a point rather than to retrieve an answer. Here are two examples:

> If you love those who love you, what reward will you get? (Matt. 5:46)

> Who of you by worrying can add a single hour to his life? (Matt. 6:27)

Jesus doesn't ask a rhetorical question to get an answer, but rather in order to make a strong statement in a creative way. The best way to approach rhetorical questions is to turn them into statements. Look at how we might transform the above examples into statements:

> You don't get any reward for loving only those who love you. (Matt. 5:46)

You can't add a single hour to your life by worrying. (Matt. 6:27)

By transforming rhetorical questions into statements you will clearly see what Jesus intended to communicate.

Parables

One of Jesus' favorite literary techniques was the parable. You're probably familiar with the stories about the good Samaritan, the lost son, the wheat and the weeds—a few of Jesus' most famous parables. A *parable* is a story with two levels of meaning, where certain details in the story represent something else (e.g., in the parable of the lost son, the father represents God). The difficulty is to know how many details in the story should stand for other things.

Throughout the centuries some Christians have taken great liberty with the parables by making almost every detail in each story stand for something. Perhaps the most famous example of such allegorization is the treatment of the parable of the good Samaritan by the early church leader Augustine.[21]

the man going down to Jericho	=	Adam
Jerusalem	=	heavenly city from which Adam fell
Jericho	=	the moon (signifying Adam's mortality)
robbers	=	the devil and his angels
stripping him	=	taking away his immortality
beating him	=	persuading him to sin
leaving him half dead	=	as a man lives, but is dead spiritually, therefore he is half dead
priest and Levite	=	priesthood and ministry of the Old Testament
the Samaritan	=	Christ himself
binding of the wounds	=	binding the restraint of sin
wine	=	exhortation to work with fervent spirit
beast	=	flesh of Christ's incarnation
the inn	=	the church
two denarii	=	promise of this life and the life to come
innkeeper	=	the apostle Paul

You can see why this approach would prove problematic.

Since the late nineteenth century a majority of New Testament scholars have insisted that every parable makes essentially one point, which usually comes at the end. This has been a welcome corrective to the allegorization used by Augustine and others. But does the "one-point rule" restrict meaning more than Jesus would have intended?

Take the parable of the lost son as an example. What is the one point? Does the one point that comes to your mind deal with the rebellious son, the resentful brother, or the forgiving father? Do you really want to pick just one and say that Jesus did not intend to make a point about the other two? The one-point approach appears to us to be inadequate. After all, not many stories of any kind make only one point.

Recently a balanced approach to interpreting the parables has been offered by the evangelical scholar Craig Blomberg.[22] Jesus' parables are not to be allegorized down to the last microscopic detail, but neither are they to be limited to only one point. Following Blomberg, we suggest two principles for interpreting Jesus' parables. (1) Look for one main point for each main character or group of characters. Most parables will make one, perhaps two, but usually not more than three main points. All the other details are there to enhance the story. Looking at the parable of the lost son (Luke 15:11–32), we can see how this interpretive guideline helps us identify three main points, one for each main character:

Rebellious son	Sinners may confess their sins and turn to God in repentance.
Forgiving father	God offers forgiveness for undeserving people.
Resentful brother	Those who claim to be God's people should not be resentful when God extends his grace to the undeserving.

(2) The main points you discover must be ones that Jesus' original audience would have understood. If we come up with a point that Jesus' audience would not grasp, we have probably missed his point. This guideline is intended to keep us from reading into Jesus' parables what he never intended in the first place.

113

Whenever we read the Gospels, we must reflect on how to apply their message to our lives. When we truly grasp God's Word, we will do more than read and interpret; we allow the great truths taught by Jesus to penetrate our hearts and minds and make a real difference in how we live.

Discussion Questions

1. How does our approach to reading the Gospels match the means of God's communication in the Gospels?
2. We often neglect to notice what the Gospel writer is trying to say to his readers by the way he puts together smaller stories. Are we really missing anything with this omission? Why or why not?
3. How is the "one-point-per-main-character" approach to the parables superior to the "one-point" approach?

Writing Assignment

Apply the two interpretive steps we used to read the Gospels to Matthew 24:43–25:13 or to another section of the Gospels selected by your teacher.

W hile we have four versions of the life and ministry of Jesus Christ (the four Gospels), we only have one account of the birth and growth of the early church. That makes Acts — our one story of the spread of Christianity across the New Testament world — unique and indispensable! This book shows us and tells us how God worked through the early church to change the world.

An important point to note is that the Gospel of Luke and the book of Acts were first written as a single work in two parts: *Luke-Acts.* Originally these two volumes even circulated among the churches as a single work, but in the second century the Gospel of Luke joined the other three Gospels and Acts began to circulate on its own.

There are some strong indications that Luke intended to link these two books closely together in telling the story. First, if you compare the opening verses of both books (Luke 1:1–4 and Acts 1:1–2), you will notice that Acts continues the same story.

Second, there are parallels between the two books. Some of the prominent themes of Luke's Gospel reoccur in Acts (e.g., prayer, the work of the Spirit, the gospel for all people). Also, both Luke and Acts feature a journey motif. In the Gospel Jesus journeys to Jerusalem and the cross (Luke 9:51; 13:22, 33; 17:11; 18:31; 19:41), while in Acts the apostles begin from Jerusalem and spread the gospel story out to the world (cf. Acts 1:8).

Third, there is a definite overlap between the ending of Luke and the beginning of Acts. Jesus' words to his disciples in Luke 24:49 are certainly fulfilled in Acts 1 – 2. When Jesus speaks about repentance and forgiveness of sins being preached in his name to all nations, beginning in Jerusalem (Luke 24:47), we automatically think of Acts 1:8. Perhaps the most noticeable overlap is the record of the ascension of Jesus in both Luke (24:51) and Acts (1:9 – 11), the only two places in the New Testament where this event is described.

Luke links his Gospel and Acts closely together as two parts of a single story. The God who acted in mighty ways in the Old Testament and revealed himself supremely in Jesus Christ is now at work by his Spirit. Luke presents to us the grand story of God's salvation. We should always remember, therefore, to read Acts as a continuation of the story that started in Luke's Gospel. What Jesus began to do during his ministry on earth he now continues to do through his Spirit-empowered followers. As a practical matter, before you study Acts, you might take time to read through the Gospel of Luke.

What Kind of Book Is Acts?

Acts Is a Story

Like the Gospels, Acts is a narrative. Because of the close connection between Luke and Acts, we can expect these two books to have much in common when it comes to literary type. That is indeed the case. Much of what we said about how to read the Gospels applies to Acts as well, including the two main interpretive questions. The primary difference is that the Gospels concentrate on one person, Jesus of Nazareth, while the story in Acts focuses on several key church leaders, mainly Peter and Paul.

Acts Is God-Centered History

As Luke widens his angle from Jesus to the early church leaders, he moves from Christ-centered biography in his Gospel to God-centered (or theological) history in Acts. Luke is a historian, who composes a reliable record of what happened in the outreach of the gospel. We should not assume, of course, that Luke approved of everything that happened. When Luke describes something that happens (e.g., Paul's quarrel with

Barnabas in Acts 15:36–40), we need to resist the temptation to turn this into the approved plan of God.

As well as being a historian, Luke is also a *theologian*, who tells his story for the purpose of advancing the Christian faith. Is it possible to be both a historian and a theologian? We believe it is. All history writing is selective (i.e., you can't possibly tell everything that happens) and is written from some faith perspective. Historians are not neutral observers without any belief system. They are human and have a point of view just like the rest of us. Their viewpoint (including their faith perspective) influences the way they interpret events, select what to include, and shape their story. In Acts, Luke gives us accurate, reliable history, but he has selected and arranged his material for theological purposes.

Luke shapes his story for theological purposes, but how are we supposed to locate theology in a story? We use many of the same principles that we used to find theological principles in the Gospels. We ask the standard narrative questions (Who? What? When? Where? Why? and How?), pay attention to instructions from the author, concentrate on direct discourse, and so on.

Perhaps the single most helpful guideline for grasping the theological truths of Acts is to look for repeated themes and patterns. In the major themes of Acts you can see Luke working out his theological purposes. When you find Luke's theological purposes, you also find the heart of his message to his original audience and to us. We turn now to survey some of the major themes in Acts.

Why Did Luke Write Acts?

Luke states his purpose for Luke-Acts in the first few verses of his Gospel: "so that you [Theophilus] may know the certainty of the things you have been taught" (Luke 1:4). Presumably Theophilus has received instruction (*katecheō*, meaning "to teach") that was not entirely adequate. Luke wants to encourage and establish Theophilus and others like him more fully in their new faith. Perhaps we should think of Acts as a kind of comprehensive discipleship manual, designed to reinforce the Christian faith for new believers. Luke does this by showing these new believers that what God promised in the Old Testament and fulfilled in Jesus, he now continues to work out. In short, the *Holy Spirit* empowers the *church* (both Jewish and Gentile believers) to take the *gospel* of Jesus Christ to the *world* (Acts 1:8).

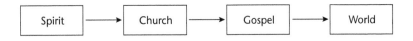

This is biblical history at its finest, painted in broad strokes to assure Christians that they are part of God's grand plan. We can hear Luke saying to believers: "You're on the right track. You're truly part of what God is doing. Don't give up!" Luke's overarching purpose surfaces in a number of subpurposes or themes. Here are a few of them.

The Holy Spirit

The whole operation starts with the Spirit of God. In Acts 1 Jesus promises that the Father will send the Holy Spirit. At Pentecost (Acts 2) the Spirit descends to indwell and empower the disciples of Jesus. The rest of the book is a record of the acts or deeds of the Spirit through the church. What Jesus began to do (as recorded in the Gospel of Luke), he continues to do through his Spirit.

God's Sovereignty

Closely related to the Spirit's role in guiding the church is the theme of God's sovereignty. When you read Acts, you are left with the strong sense that God is in control. The Old Testament Scriptures are fulfilled as God works out his plan (e.g., Acts 1:16; 2:16–21, 25–28, 34–35; 4:24–25; 13:32–37, 47). God's will has been accomplished through Jesus (2:23–24) and his purpose is being accomplished through his people.

The Church

The Spirit works chiefly through the church (the people of God) to accomplish his will. As the summaries in Acts 2:42–47 and 4:32–35 illustrate, the Spirit creates a healthy, thriving community where people worship God, care for each other, grow spiritually, and join in the mission.

Prayer

As in the Gospel of Luke, prayer is a major theme in Acts. The early Christians were marked as people of prayer, and you will find them praying in almost every chapter of Acts.

Suffering

As we read about wonderful things that God is doing in Acts, we sometimes lose sight of the price paid by the early Christians. They suffer imprisonment, beatings, and rejection; they face angry mobs, violent storms, persecution, and even death (e.g., 5:41; 7:59–60; 9:15–16; 12:4; 14:22; 16:22–23; 20:23–24; 21:30–33; 27:13–44). In spite of such hardships, the gospel advances.

Gentiles

In Acts the gospel comes first to the Jews, but spreads quickly to the "ends of the earth" — to Gentile country. (A *Gentile* is anyone who is not an ethnic Jew.) The true Israel of God is made up of Jews *and* Gentiles who have accepted Jesus the Messiah. In his Pentecostal sermon Peter quotes the prophet Joel, who says, "I will pour out my Spirit on *all people* ... and *everyone* who calls on the name of the Lord will be saved" (2:17b, 21, italics added). Peter later realizes that God is serious about a mission that includes Gentiles (8:14–17; 10:1–48). The narrative movement in Acts is from Jerusalem to Rome, from Peter to Paul, from Jew only to Jew and Gentile.

Witness

The apostles focus their witness on the resurrection of Jesus from the dead (e.g., 1:8, 22; 2:32–36; 4:2, 20, 33; 5:20, 32, 42; 10:39–41). The empowering of the Spirit for witness does not stop with the original apostles (e.g., Peter, Stephen, Philip, Paul). Luke's message in Acts is clear: To be a follower of Jesus Christ means to be a faithful witness.

Grasping the Message of Acts

Since Acts is narrative, we should approach it in much the same way that we approached the Gospels. The two interpretive questions remain central. (1) What is the central message of each episode? (2) What is Luke telling his readers by the way he puts the individual stories and speeches together to form the larger narrative?

To find theological principles in the individual episodes of Acts, we should focus on the standard narrative questions: Who? What? When? Where? Why? and How? These provide a simple plan for understanding any story. When looking for theological principles in a series of episodes, look for connections between the stories. How are the stories positioned? What does the length of each episode tell us about what Luke thinks is important? Above all, what themes and patterns are repeated throughout Acts?

When reading and applying Acts, we face one major interpretive challenge that we did not have to deal with when reading the Gospels, even though both are narrative. In the Gospels we read about Jesus and his original disciples without ever once thinking that we will be in that same situation. We will never get into a boat with Jesus to cross the Sea of Galilee or walk with him through the streets of Jerusalem. In Acts, however, the situation is different. From the Gospels to Acts there is a major shift in biblical history from the period of Jesus' ministry on earth to the period of the Spirit's ministry through the church. And as believing readers, we are part of that Spirit-driven church!

Here comes the tricky part. Should we take Acts as *normative* so that the church of all times should imitate the experiences and practices of the early church? Or should we read Acts as merely *descriptive* of what was valuable and inspiring in the early church, but not necessarily binding on us today? Without a doubt this is the most significant issue we face as we learn to interpret Acts. On the one hand, if we read Acts as purely descriptive, why bother reading it at all? If, on the other hand, we take Acts as normative, do we have to repeat *all* the practices of the early church, including the rivalries, immoralities, and heresies? Do we have to make decisions by casting lots? Do we have to pool our possessions?

Will God judge us like he judged Ananias and Sapphira (sudden death for lying)? Should we read Acts as normative or descriptive?

In making the Interpretive Journey in the book of Acts, we believe that a *both-and* approach works best (i.e., take some parts of Acts as normative and other parts as descriptive). The difficulty lies in knowing what is normative for the church today and what is not. On what basis should we make these decisions? Unless we think through this issue, we will almost certainly pick and choose based on how we feel at the time. We offer the following guidelines for determining what in Acts is normative for today's church.[23]

First, look for what Luke intended to communicate to his readers (e.g., by finding common themes and patterns that connect the stories). When we find the message Luke has intended, we find the normative meaning of the passage.

Second, look for positive and negative examples in the characters of the story. Luke likely intends for what is done by the positive characters throughout Acts to be taken as normative, although we should admit to the unique role played by the apostles at this stage of salvation history.

Third, read individual passages in light of the overall story of Acts and the rest of the New Testament. In some cases the progression of the whole story will offer clear boundaries for determining what is normative in specific passages. We should not claim as normative any interpretation that fails to honor the overall movement of the story (e.g., seeing a two-stage conversion as normative from Acts 19:1–7).

Fourth, look to other parts of Acts to clarify what is normative. We know, for example, that Acts doesn't teach communal living as normative by reading Acts 2 and 4 in light of Acts 5, where sharing possessions is clearly voluntary. What is normative in all three chapters is radical generosity.

Fifth, perhaps the most important principle for identifying what is normative for the church today is to look for themes and patterns that remain constant throughout the changing story of Acts. Earlier we identified a number of general themes in Acts: the work of the Spirit, God's sovereignty, the role of the church, prayer, suffering, the gospel for Jews and Gentiles, and the power of witness. These represent normative realities for the church throughout the ages.

Conclusion

God gave us four accounts of the one story of Jesus Christ — Matthew, Mark, Luke, and John. As we take the Gospels through the Interpretive Journey, we ask two basic questions: (1) What is the main message of each episode? (2) What is the Gospel writer trying to communicate by the way he puts the smaller stories together? In this way we are able to read individual stories as well as a whole series of stories.

Much the same is true for that great adventure called Acts. What Jesus began to do during his ministry on earth, he now continues to do as his Spirit empowers the church to take the gospel to the world. The most difficult problem when reading Acts is knowing how to deal with the river of differences and identify what is normative for today's church. We have suggested some guidelines for doing so. Our prayer is that what we have said will encourage you to be a more faithful interpreter of this powerful story of the birth and growth of the early church.

We also learned in this chapter that interpreting Scripture does not stop when we cross the river of differences between the biblical audience and today. We must wrestle with how to apply the great truths of the Gospels and Acts to our lives. Developing legitimate applications of some principles will be straightforward and rather easy; for others it will be complex and difficult. In the end, we can be grateful that we have the good news of Jesus and the story of the early church written down so that we may pick up the book at any time and read and apply it.

Discussion Questions

1. Which of the main themes in Acts mentioned in this chapter does your church need to focus on most at this point in its journey?
2. What additional themes do you see repeated consistently throughout Acts?
3. Do you prefer to interpret Acts as normative or descriptive? Why?

Writing Assignment

Take one of the following texts through the four steps of the Interpretive Journey:

- Acts 2:42–47
- Acts 6:1–7
- Acts 13:1–3
- Acts 15:1–21
- Acts 17:16–34

*D*o you remember the first time that you read (or tried to read) Revelation? What kind of experience was it? Confusing? Intimidating? Exhilarating? Mind-boggling? You probably made sense of chapter 1 and may have even felt comfortable with the messages to the seven churches in chapters 2 and 3. But how did you react to the four living creatures in chapter 4 or the Lamb with seven horns and eyes in chapter 5? Or what did you think about the moon turning red or the 144,000 or the talking eagle or Babylon, the mother of prostitutes? If you are like most people, when you finished the last page, you put down your Bible and concluded that Revelation is one bizarre book.

This last book of the Bible describes itself as a "revelation of Jesus Christ" (1:1), an expression that functions as a title for the entire book. The term *revelation* (*apokalypsis* in Greek) suggests that something once hidden is now being unveiled or displayed openly (i.e., from John's generation on).

In this "final chapter" of the story of salvation, God pulls back the curtain to give his people a glimpse of his plans for human history, plans that center around Jesus Christ. Revelation is powerful, difficult, perplexing, colorful, suspenseful, tragic, and amazing. It is like a raging river, a bloody battle, an enticing mystery, and a breathtaking wedding all rolled into one. You had better fasten your seat belt because Revelation will take you on the interpretive ride of your life.

What Is the Purpose of Revelation?

The purpose of Revelation is tied up with its literary type as a prophetic-apocalyptic letter, especially with its use of images. The images of Revelation create a symbolic world in which the readers may live as they read (or hear) the book. As they enter this symbolic world, its message affects them and changes their entire perception of the world in which they live. They can see their own situation from a heavenly perspective.

Revelation uses images to answer the question, "Who is Lord?" During times of oppression and persecution, the righteous suffer and the wicked seem to prosper. This raises concerns about whether God is still on his throne and in control. Revelation says that in spite of how things appear, Caesar is not Lord and Satan is not Lord. Rather, Jesus is Lord and he is coming soon to set things right.

God uses this prophetic-apocalyptic letter to pull back the curtain in his cosmic drama and show his people how things will turn out in the end. Its main message is "God will win!" Those who are not compromising with the pagan world should see God's future and be filled with hope in the present. But those who are compromising should be shocked out of their spiritual slumber and warned to repent. As the "last chapter" of the story of salvation, Revelation gives people a foretaste of God's ultimate victory and offers them the perspective and the encouragement they need to overcome.

Interpreting Revelation

General Approaches to Revelation

Interpreters have traditionally approached Revelation in five primary ways. The *preterist* approach attempts to understand Revelation only in the way that John's original audience would have understood it. The *historicist* approach views Revelation as an outline of what has happened throughout church history from the first century until the return of Christ. The *futurist* approach views most of the book as related to future events immediately preceding the end of history. The *idealist* approach does not understand Revelation in terms of any particular reference to time, but rather relates it to the ongoing struggle between good and evil.

Finally, many scholars today opt for an *eclectic* approach to reading Revelation because it seeks to combine the strengths of several of the above approaches. For example, we should read Revelation the same way that we read every other book of the Bible—by taking its historical context seriously. Revelation also presents timeless truths for surviving the struggle between good and evil (e.g., forsake complacency and persevere during times of persecution). Moreover, this book certainly has something to say about events still to come. Some events it describes await future fulfillment (e.g., the return of Christ, great white throne judgment, and the arrival of the new heaven and new earth).

Specific Principles for Reading Revelation

In addition to these general approaches to Revelation, we need more specific principles for reading this remarkable prophetic-apocalyptic letter. Here are seven suggestions.[24]

1. Read Revelation with humility. We should resist "Revelation-made-easy" approaches because Revelation is not easy! We should beware of "experts" who claim absolute knowledge about every minute detail of this book. Reading with a humble mind means that we are willing to change our view when the biblical evidence points in a different direction.

2. Try to discover the message to the original readers. When it comes to reading Revelation, the tendency is to ignore the first Christians and jump directly to God's message for us. This approach implies that in Revelation God was not really speaking to the first Christians and betrays an interpretive arrogance on our part. What if Christ does not return until AD 4000? Would Revelation still have a message for us since we would not be the last generation?

We must never forget that the first Christians were blessed for obeying Revelation (1:3) and that the book is described as an unsealed (or open) book, even for people living in John's day (22:10). The best place to begin is with the question: "What is John trying to communicate to his audience?" If our interpretation makes no sense for original readers, we have probably missed the meaning of the passage. The Interpretive Journey serves as a reminder that we must understand what it *meant* in John's day in order to understand what it *means* today.

3. Don't try to discover a strict chronological map of future events. Don't look for Revelation to progress in a neat linear fashion. The visions of the book serve to make a dramatic impact on the reader rather than present a precise chronological sequence of future events. For example, notice that the sixth seal (6:12 – 17) takes us to the end of the age. But when the seventh seal is opened, we are given a whole new set of judgments — the trumpets — and the seventh trumpet (11:15 – 19) also takes us to the end of the age. Then with the first bowl in 16:1 – 2 we are given another series of judgments. Revelation 19 – 22 paints the most colorful and detailed picture of the end, but as you can see, this is not the first time the readers have been transported to the very end. Rather than searching for a chronological map of future events in Revelation, we encourage you to grasp the main message in each vision about living in the here and now.

4. Take Revelation seriously, but don't always take it literally. Some who say that we should interpret Scripture symbolically do so in order to deny the reality of a scriptural truth or a historical event. That is not our intention. We insist that picture language with its symbols, images, and figures is capable of conveying literal truth and describing literal, historical events. Picture language is just another language vehicle, another way of communicating reality. In our way of thinking, Revelation uses picture language to emphasize historical reality rather than to deny or diminish it.

Since our interpretive method should match the literary genre used by the biblical author, we should avoid taking picture language literally. When we try to force a literal method on picture language, we run the risk of perverting the author's intended meaning. For example, what happens when we try to take the reference in Revelation 17:9 to the woman who sits on seven hills literally? First-century Christians would naturally have understood the woman to represent Rome, a city built on seven hills. The text probably also looks beyond Rome to powerful pagan empires opposed to God. We take picture language seriously, but not literally.

5. Pay attention when John identifies an image. When John himself provides a clue to the interpretation of an image, we should take notice. For example, in Revelation 1:17 the Son of Man is Christ, in 1:20 the golden lampstands are the churches, in 5:5 – 6 the Lion is the Lamb, in 12:9 the dragon is Satan, and in 21:9 – 10 the heavenly Jerusalem is the wife of the Lamb or the church. When images that John has identified are repeated later in the book, we should assume that they probably refer to the same things (e.g., the lampstands in 1:20 and in 11:3–4).

But don't confuse John's direct identification of an image (those mentioned above) with John's fluid use of images. In other words, John is not shy about using the same image to refer to different things. For example, the seven stars are the angels of the seven churches (1:16, 20; 2:1; 3:1). But John also uses the image of a star (not the seven stars) to refer to other things, such as God's agents of judgment (8:10–12) or even Jesus himself (22:16). Even though John is free to use images to refer to different things, when he identifies an image directly, we should pay attention.

6. *Look to the Old Testament and historical context when interpreting images and symbols.* One of the most difficult aspects of reading Revelation is knowing what the symbols refer to. In other words, we usually know what Revelation is saying, but we are often not sure what it is talking about. The two places to go for wisdom are to the historical context and to the Old Testament. Revelation is filled with numerous echoes and allusions to the Old Testament. In fact, Revelation contains more Old Testament references than any other New Testament book, especially references to Psalms, Isaiah, Ezekiel, and Daniel. As you study the historical context and the Old Testament context, you can make more sense of the images used in Revelation.

7. *Above all, focus on the main idea and don't press all the details.* This last interpretive guideline is perhaps the most important of all. With most literary genres in the Bible, we begin with the details and build our way toward an understanding of the whole. With Revelation, however, we should start with the big picture and work toward an understanding of the details. As we seek to identify theological principles in Revelation, we should focus on the main ideas. Resist the temptation to focus on the smallest details. Stay focused on the main point of each section or vision.

Conclusion

In Revelation, God pulls back the curtain to give his people a glimpse of his plans for human history. Center stage in this cosmic drama is Jesus

Christ, the Lion and the Lamb, who secures victory through sacrifice. Revelation is strange because of its blended literary genre (prophetic-apocalyptic letter), but it is not a closed book. We can grasp the meaning of Revelation and apply it to our lives, but we need to "play by its rules," not our own.

Discussion Questions

1. Of the primary approaches to interpreting Revelation, which one do you prefer? Why?
2. Which of the seven suggestions for reading Revelation seems most helpful to you?
3. Why do Christians of every age need to hear the message of Revelation? In other words, what are we missing when we ignore this book?

Writing Assignment

Read the entire book of Revelation and write a one-line description of the main idea of each chapter of the book. For example, for Revelation 1 you might write, "John's vision of the glorified Christ among the churches."

Old Testament — Law

13

The Old Testament and the Interpretive Journey

Before we venture into the specifics of Old Testament law, we need to revisit our understanding of the Interpretive Journey. Now that you are a veteran of many Interpretive Journeys, you are ready to tackle the Old Testament. In this chapter and in chapters 14 and 15 you will take all that you have learned so far in this book and apply it to the various genres of the Old Testament. You will learn how to interpret and apply Old Testament legal material, prophetic writings, and the psalms. The interpretive river in the Old Testament is usually wider than the one in the New Testament, and the principlizing bridge becomes even more critical. The genre differences are also significant, as you will see. However, the stories and poems in the Old Testament are exciting and inspiring, and God reveals many things about himself through these texts. Without doubt, the time you spend in the Old Testament will be rewarding.

Also, keep in mind that we must read and interpret the Old Testament as Christians. That is, although we believe that the Old Testament is part of God's inspired Word to us, we do not want to ignore the Cross and thus interpret and apply this literature as if we were Old Testament Hebrews. We affirm that we are New Testament Christians, and we will interpret the Old Testament from that vantage point.

During Step 1 of the Interpretive Journey (*Grasp the text in their town*), of course, we will focus on what the text meant to those living in the Old Testament era. However, it is critical that we not stop here! After we have defined the width of the river (Step 2) and formulated a theological principle (Step 3), we need to insert a new step. Before we move to application, we want to run the theological principle through the grid of the New Testament, looking for what the New Testament adds to that principle or how the New Testament modifies it. Thus, while the Interpretive Journey has remained a four-step journey throughout the New Testament, it will expand to a five-step journey in the Old Testament. We will explain this extra step in more detail in the chapters to come, but we want to introduce you to the concept here.

The Old Testament Interpretive Journey, therefore, will now look like this:

Step 1: Grasp the text in their town. What did the text mean to the biblical audience?

Step 2: Measure the width of the river to cross. What are the differences between the biblical audience and us?

Step 3: Cross the principlizing bridge. What is the theological principle of this text?

Step 4: Cross into the New Testament. Does the New Testament teaching modify or qualify this principle, and if so, how?

Step 5: Grasp the text in our town. How should individual Christians today apply the theological principle in their lives?

Law: Introduction

A large portion of the Pentateuch (the first five books of the Bible) is comprised of *laws*. Indeed, there are over six hundred commandments in these books. We find this legal material throughout most of Leviticus and most of Deuteronomy. Also, about half of Exodus along with a portion of Numbers presents various laws that God gave to Israel. Obviously, these laws are important. But many of them seem strange to us — even weird. Consider the following laws:

Exodus 34:26: "Do not cook a young goat in his mother's milk."
Leviticus 19:19: "Do not wear clothing woven of two kinds of material."

Leviticus 13:40: "When a man has lost his hair and is bald, he is clean."

Furthermore, there are numerous Old Testament laws that we as modern Christians violate with some regularity. Which of the following have you violated?

Deuteronomy 22:5: "A woman must not wear men's clothing, nor a man wear woman's clothing."
Leviticus 19:28: "Do not ... put tattoo marks on yourselves."
Deuteronomy 14:8: "The pig is also unclean; although it has a split hoof, it does not chew the cud. You are not to eat their meat or touch their carcasses."

While we tend to ignore such laws, there are other Old Testament commands that we latch onto as the moral underpinnings of Christian behavior. These will be more familiar to you:

Leviticus 19:18: "Love your neighbor as yourself."
Exodus 20:13: "You shall not murder."
Deuteronomy 5:18: "You shall not commit adultery."

So, why do we adhere to some laws and ignore others? Which laws are valid and which are not? Many Christians today are baffled by the interpretive problem of the law. Some of us take the approach of simply skimming through the legal texts and skipping over all the laws that do not seem to apply to us. These laws we choose to ignore altogether. Then when we encounter one that does seem to make sense in today's world, we grab it, underline it, and use it as a guideline for living. Surely this willy-nilly approach to interpreting the Old Testament law is inadequate. But how should we interpret the law?

Law: The Narrative Context

The Old Testament legal material does not appear in isolation. The Old Testament law is firmly embedded into the story of Israel's theological history. It is part of the narrative that runs from Genesis 12 to 2 Kings 25.

The law is not presented by itself as some sort of timeless universal code. Rather, it is presented as part of the theological narrative that describes how God delivered Israel from Egypt and established them in the Promised Land as his people.

The Old Testament law, therefore, is an integral part of the story of Israel's exodus, wandering, and conquest. Our interpretive approach to the law should take this into account. Remember the importance of *context* that you learned back in chapter 6. The law is part of a story, and this story provides an important context for interpreting the law.

Law: The Covenant Context

God introduces the law in a covenant context, saying, "Now if you obey me fully and keep my covenant, then out of all nations you will be my treasured possession" (Ex. 19:5). The people agree to keep the terms of the covenant (24:3), and Moses seals the agreement in blood: "Moses then took the blood, sprinkled it on the people and said, 'This is the blood of the covenant that the LORD has made with you in accordance with all these words'" (24:8).

Part of this covenant was God's promise to dwell in Israel's midst. This is stressed several times in the latter half of Exodus (Ex. 25:8; 29:45; 34:14 – 17; 40:34 – 38). Associated with God's presence are the instructions for constructing the ark and the tabernacle, the place where God will dwell (Ex. 25 – 31; 35 – 40). Leviticus is thus the natural sequel to the latter half of Exodus, for it addresses how Israel is to live with God in their midst. How do they approach him? How do they deal with personal and national sin before a holy God living among them? How do they worship and fellowship with this holy, awesome God in their midst? Leviticus provides the answers to these questions, giving practical guidelines for living with God in their midst under the terms of the Mosaic covenant.

After Israel's refusal to obey God and enter the Promised Land (Numbers 13 – 14), God sends them into the desert for thirty-eight more years to allow that disobedient generation to die out. God then leads the people back toward Canaan. Before they enter, however, he calls them to a covenant renewal. With this new, younger generation, he reinstates the

Mosaic covenant that he originally made with their parents in the book of Exodus. Deuteronomy describes this renewed call to covenant that God is making with Israel just prior to their entering the Promised Land. Indeed, in Deuteronomy God elaborates and gives even more details about the covenant than he did in Exodus. Deuteronomy describes in detail the terms by which Israel will be able to live in the Promised Land successfully and be blessed by God.

Since the Old Testament law is tightly intertwined into the Mosaic covenant, it is important to make several observations about the nature of this covenant.

1. The Mosaic covenant is closely associated with Israel's conquest and occupation of the land of Canaan. The covenant provides the framework by which Israel can occupy and live prosperously with God in the Promised Land. The close connection between the covenant and the land is stressed over and over in Deuteronomy.

2. The blessings from the Mosaic covenant are conditional. A constant warning runs throughout Deuteronomy, explaining to Israel that obedience to the covenant will bring blessing but disobedience to the covenant will bring punishment and curses. Deuteronomy 28 is particularly explicit in this regard: Verses 1–14 list the blessings for Israel if they obey the terms of the covenant (the law) while verses 15–68 spell out the terrible consequences if they do not.

3. The Mosaic covenant is no longer a functional covenant. New Testament believers are no longer under the old, Mosaic covenant. Hebrews 8–9 makes it clear that Jesus came as the mediator of a *new* covenant, which replaced the *old* covenant. "By calling this covenant 'new,' he has made the first one obsolete" (Heb. 8:13). The Old Testament law presented the terms by which Israel could receive blessings in the land under the old (Mosaic) covenant. If the old covenant is no longer valid, how can the laws that made up that covenant still be valid? If the old covenant is obsolete, should we not also view the system of laws that comprise the old covenant as obsolete?

4. The Old Testament law as part of the Mosaic covenant is no longer applicable over us as law. Paul makes it clear that Christians are not under the Old Testament law. For example, in Galatians 2:15–16 he writes, "We

... know that a man is not justified by observing the law, but by faith in Jesus Christ." In Romans 7:4 Paul states that "you also died to the law through the body of Christ." Likewise, in Galatians 3:25 he declares, "Now that faith has come, we are no longer under the supervision of the law."

Paul argues forcefully against Christians returning to the Old Testament law. In our interpretation and application of the law, we must be cautious to heed Paul's admonition. Now that we are freed from the law through Christ, we do not want to put people back under the law through our interpretive method.

But what about Matthew 5:17, where Jesus states, "Do not think that I have come to abolish the Law or the Prophets; I have not come to abolish them but to fulfill them"? Is Jesus contradicting Paul? We do not think so. First of all, note that the phrase "the Law and the Prophets" is a reference to the entire Old Testament. So Jesus is not just speaking about the Mosaic law. Also note that the antithesis is not between *abolish* and *observe,* but between *abolish* and *fulfill.* Jesus does not claim that he has come to *observe* the law or to *keep* the law; rather, he has come to *fulfill* it.

Matthew uses the Greek word translated as "fulfill" numerous times; it normally means "to bring to its intended meaning." Jesus is *not* stating that the law is eternally binding on New Testament believers. If that were the case, we would be required to keep the sacrificial and ceremonial laws as well as the moral ones. This is clearly against New Testament teaching. What Jesus is saying is that he did not come to sweep away the righteous demands of the law, but that he came to fulfill these righteous demands.

5. We must interpret the law through the grid of New Testament teaching. Second Timothy 3:16 tells us that "all Scripture is God-breathed and is useful for teaching, rebuking, correcting and training in righteousness." Paul certainly is including the law in his phrase "all Scripture." As part of God's Word, the value of the Old Testament law is eternal. We should study and seek to apply all of it.

However, the law no longer functions as the terms of the covenant for us, and thus it no longer applies as direct, literal law for us. The coming of Christ as the fulfillment of the law has changed that forever. However, the Old Testament legal material does contain rich *principles* and *lessons* for living that are still relevant when interpreted through New Testament teaching.

6. The best method for interpreting the law is to follow the Interpretive Journey. After the observation phase of study, we determine what the text meant to the biblical audience. Then we identify the differences between the biblical audience and us. Next, we cross the principlizing bridge and draw out theological principles. We take the theological principles and filter them through the grid of New Testament teaching as we cross over into the New Testament to identify the meaning for today's Christian audience. Finally we determine specific applications of this meaning that will apply to specific individuals today.

This approach allows us to interpret all Old Testament narrative texts and legal texts with the same methodology. It provides us with a step-by-step system by which we can find valid application for a wide range of Old Testament stories and laws. Are you ready to tackle the Old Testament law on your own?

Discussion Questions

1. Why is the "willy-nilly" approach to interpreting Old Testament law inadequate?
2. How does the covenant context of the law affect our approach to interpreting law?
3. What is the most significant insight you have gained from this chapter about interpreting Old Testament law?

Writing Assignment

For each passage below, first, study the text and make as many observations as you can. Mark the observations on a photocopy of the text. Be sure that you understand the meanings of all of the words. Do background study as needed to understand each term. Next, identify the historical-cultural and the literary context. When and where is this law given? What does the surrounding text discuss? Finally, apply the Interpretive Journey to the text by completing the following:

Step 1: Grasp the text in their town. What did the text mean to the biblical audience?

Step 2: Measure the width of the river to cross. What are the differences between the biblical audience and us?

Step 3: Cross the principlizing bridge. What is the theological principle in this text?

Step 4: Cross into the New Testament. Does the New Testament teaching modify or qualify this principle, and if so, how?

Step 5: Grasp the text in our town. How should individual Christians today apply the modified theological principle in their lives?

Leviticus 26:1: Do not make idols or set up an image of a sacred stone

for yourselves, and do not place a carved stone in your land to bow down

before it. I am the LORD your God.

Leviticus 23:22: When you reap the harvest of your land, do not reap

to the very edges of your field or gather the gleanings of your harvest.

Leave them for the poor and the alien. I am the LORD your God.

*T*he Prophets! What a fantastic collection of books! The prophetic books of the Old Testament contain some of the most inspiring passages in the Bible. Isaiah is a favorite of many Christians. Recall his uplifting words in Isaiah 40:31:

> But those who hope in the LORD
>> will renew their strength.
> They will soar on wings like eagles;
>> they will run and not grow weary,
>> they will walk and not be faint.

Christians love that verse. Doesn't it lift your heart? We could go on and on, citing wonderful, beloved prophetic passages.

The Prophets, however, also contain some rather unusual and difficult verses. For example, there are some gruesome texts, such as Amos 3:12:

> As a shepherd saves from the lion's mouth
>> only two leg bones or a piece of an ear,
>> so will the Israelites be saved.

Some of the Old Testament prophetic passages are wonderful and easy to grasp, but some texts are bewildering and troubling. In this chapter we will teach you how to tackle this fascinating portion of Scripture.

The Nature of Old Testament Prophetic Literature

A large percentage of the latter half of the Old Testament is comprised of prophetic literature. Indeed, the Prophets take up as much space in the Bible as the New Testament does! Clearly, then, this material is an important part of God's message to us.

The prophetic books contain primarily numerous short-spoken or preached messages, usually proclaimed by the prophet to either the nation of Israel or the nation of Judah. They also contain visions from God, short narrative sections, and symbolic acts.

Only a small percentage of Old Testament prophecy deals with events that are still future to us. This may surprise you. Many people assume that the term *prophecy* only refers to events of the end times and that the prophets of the Old Testament are primarily concerned with predicting the end times. Note, however, what Fee and Stuart write: "Less than 2 percent of Old Testament prophecy is messianic. Less than 5 percent specifically describes the new-covenant age. Less than 1 percent concerns events yet to come in our time."[25] The vast majority of the material in the prophetic books addresses the disobedience of Israel and/or Judah and their consequential impending judgment. The role of the prophet includes the proclamation of this disobedience and the imminent judgment as much as it does the prediction of things to come in the more distant future.

The Prophets use poetry for much of their message, and it is the poetic aspect of their message that is the most foreign to us. A central feature of Hebrew poetry is the extensive use of *figures of speech*. These figures of speech are some of the main weapons in the literary arsenal of the prophets. Such language is what makes the prophetic books so colorful and fascinating. Note, for example:

- Amos does not simply say, "God is mad." Rather, he proclaims, "The lion has roared" (Amos 3:8).
- Isaiah does not analytically contrast the awfulness of sin and the amazing wonder of forgiveness; he uses figurative language, announcing, "Though your sins are like scarlet, they shall be as white as snow" (Isa. 1:18).

- Jeremiah is disgusted with Judah's unfaithful attitude toward God and wants to convey the pain the Lord feels because Judah has left him for idols. Thus, throughout the book he compares Judah to an unfaithful wife who has become a prostitute: "You have lived as a prostitute with many lovers" (Jer. 3:1).

The power of poetry lies in its ability to affect the emotions of the reader or listener. Without doubt, prophetic literature is the most emotional literature in the Bible. The prophets express the deep, deep love of the Lord toward his people and the intense pain he feels as a result of their rejection of him. Nevertheless, the prophets are also explicit in their description of how horrible the coming judgment (invasion by the Assyrians or Babylonians) will be. They are scathing in their critique and criticism of society, especially of the king and the corrupt priesthood.

Another important feature to note about the prophets is that their books are primarily *anthologies*. By this we mean that the prophetic books are collections of shorter units, usually oral messages that the prophets have proclaimed publicly to the people of Israel or Judah. Other literary units, such as narrative, oracles, and visions, are mixed in. Sometimes the delivered oral message is the vision or oracle.

It is important to note the *collection* nature of the books. Like a contemporary collection of a writer's poetry, the prophetic books contain relatively independent, shorter units. These units are not usually arranged chronologically, and often they do not appear to have thematic order either (see especially Jeremiah). Occasionally a broad overall theme (judgment, deliverance) will unite a large section of text, but for the most part, tight thematic unity is absent.

The Historical-Cultural and Theological Contexts

In chapters 5 and 6 we learned how important historical-cultural and literary contexts are to proper interpretation. Since the Old Testament prophetic literature is unique, to attempt to interpret it out of context is to invite confusion and error. First of all, we must identify the historical-cultural context in which the prophets preached.

The books of 1 and 2 Kings tell the story of how the two nations of the Hebrews, Israel and Judah, continually fall away from the Lord, turning instead to the idols of their neighbors. Ultimately the Lord punishes them, and they lose the right to live in the Promised Land. The northern kingdom, Israel, falls into idolatry early and is destroyed by the Assyrians (722 BC). Later, the southern kingdom, Judah, likewise turns away and is destroyed by the Babylonians (587 BC). The book of 2 Kings ends with the destruction of Jerusalem and the exile of the southern kingdom's inhabitants to Babylon.

The prophets preach primarily within the context of the later part of this story. As the nation turns away from the Lord, thus forgetting the covenant agreement they made with God in Exodus and Deuteronomy, the prophets emerge as God's spokesmen to call the people back to covenant obedience. Thus, in regard to the historical context, most of the prophets preach in one of two contexts: just prior to the Assyrian invasion, which destroyed the northern kingdom, Israel; or just prior to the Babylonian invasion, which destroyed the southern kingdom, Judah.

These contexts are important in order to understand the prophets. We must constantly keep them before us as we read and interpret the Old Testament prophetic literature. Theologically the prophets proclaim their message from the context of the Mosaic covenant, primarily as defined in Deuteronomy. They tell the people to repent, to turn from idols, and to return to the covenant they agreed to keep in Deuteronomy. They warn the Israelites of the terrible punishments God threatened in Deuteronomy. The ultimate punishment, which they announce with sorrow, is the loss of God's presence and the loss of the Promised Land.

The Basic Prophetic Message

Writing in the historical context of an imminent invasion by either the Assyrians or the Babylonians, the prophets serve as the Lord's prosecuting attorneys. They stand before the Lord, accusing and warning the people of the consequences of covenant violation. While there are numerous nuances and subpoints to their proclamation, their overall message can be boiled down to three basic points, each of which is important to the message of the prophets:

1. You have broken the covenant; you had better repent!
2. No repentance? Then judgment!

3. Yet there is hope beyond the judgment for a glorious, future restoration.

1. You have broken the covenant; you had better repent! The prophets stress how serious the nation's covenant violation has become and the extent to which the people have shattered the covenant. They present much evidence validating this charge. This evidence falls into three categories, three main areas of covenant violation, all of which are explicitly listed in Deuteronomy: idolatry, social injustice, and religious ritualism.

a. Idolatry. Idolatry is the most flagrant violation of the covenant, and the prophets preach continuously against it. The northern kingdom of Israel engages in idolatry from their political beginning, with the golden calves in Bethel and Dan. Idolatry is not merely a violation of the law. It strikes at the heart of the relationship between the Lord and his people. The central covenant formula in the Old Testament is the statement by the Lord that "I will be your God; you will be my people. I will dwell in your midst." Idolatry rejects this relationship. Several prophets stress the emotional hurt that God feels at this rejection. For God the issue is as much a relational issue as a legal one.

b. Social injustice. The covenant in Deuteronomy, however, bound the people to more than just the worship of the Lord. Relationship with God required proper relationship with people. The Lord was concerned with social justice for all, and he was especially concerned with how weaker individuals in society were treated. Deuteronomy demanded fair treatment of workers (Deut. 24:14ff.), justice in the court system (19:15–21), and special care for widows, orphans, and foreigners (24:17–22). As Israel and Judah turn from the Lord, they also turn from the Lord's demands for social justice. The prophets consistently condemn this and cite it as a central part of the covenant violation. They frequently cite the treatment of orphans and widows as examples of the social failure of the people; this lack of social justice also invalidates the sacrifices.

c. Religious ritualism. The nation is relying on religious ritualism instead of relationship. The people have forgotten that ritual is the means to the relationship, not a substitute for relationship. As Israel becomes more enamored with formalized ritual, they lose the concept of relationship with the Lord. They trivialize the significance of his Presence in their midst. They think that only ritual is required of them. They draw the illogical conclusion that proper ritual will cover over other covenant violations like social injustice and idolatry. They rationalize their social injustice and their syncretism by focusing on the cultic ritual. This is hypocritical, the prophets declare, and not at all what God wants. Micah states this clearly in Micah 6:7–8:

> Will the LORD be pleased with thousands of rams,
> with ten thousand rivers of oil?
> Shall I offer up my firstborn for my transgression,
> the fruit of my body for the sin of my soul?
> He has showed you, O man, what is good.
> And what does the LORD require of you?
> To act justly and to love mercy
> and to walk humbly with your God.

Likewise, in Isaiah 1:11–13a the Lord asks, "The multitude of your sacrifices, what are they to me?... Who has asked this of you, this trampling of my courts? Stop bringing meaningless offerings."

Idolatry, social injustice, and religious ritualism — these are the three interrelated indictments that make up one aspect of point 1 of the prophetic message. The call to repent is the other aspect. The prophets beg the people to repent and to restore their relationship with the Lord. Even after the prophets proclaim that the judgment is imminent, they continue to plead for repentance.

2. No repentance? Then judgment! Neither Israel nor Judah repents, and the prophets acknowledge that obstinacy, proclaiming the severe consequences. Much of the material in the prophetic books delineates the terrible imminent judgment about to fall on Israel or Judah. The major judgments predicted by the prophets are the horrific invasions by the Assyrians and the Babylonians. The most serious aspect of this is the loss of the Promised Land. The Lord is about to drive his people out of the Promised Land, as he warned in Deuteronomy.

3. Yet there is hope beyond the judgment for a glorious, future restoration. The messianic promises and future predictions of the prophets comprise a large portion of this point. The prophets do not proclaim a restoration after the destruction that simply returns back to the current status quo. The theological and relational picture of God's people in the future is different—and better. In the future, the prophets proclaim, there will be a new exodus (Isaiah), a new covenant (Jeremiah), and a new presence of the Lord's indwelling spirit (Ezekiel and Joel). Forgiveness and peace will characterize this new system. Relationship will replace ritual.

All of the wonderful prophecies of Christ fall into this category. The prophets announce that the people have failed miserably to keep the law and the Mosaic covenant. However, after the destruction there will be a glorious restoration that includes the non-Jewish peoples (Gentiles). The Messiah will come and inaugurate a new and better covenant. Furthermore, these events are not haphazard, nor are they driven by chance or by the determination of world nations. Quite to the contrary, the prophets proclaim boldly, the judgment and the restoration are part of God's plan, and the unfolding of these events provides clear evidence that he is the Lord over history.

Most of the prophets can be summarized by these three points. For example, Isaiah, Jeremiah, Ezekiel, Hosea, Micah, and Zephaniah contain all three points. Amos focuses primarily only on points 1 and 2 (broken covenant and judgment); not until chapter 8 does he mention any future hope and restoration. Joel, by contrast, virtually skips point 1, apparently assuming that the people understand that they have broken the covenant. He goes straight into judgment (point 2) and then into the future restoration (point 3).

Obadiah and Nahum do not follow the typical pattern at all. They are different because they preach against foreign nations (Edom and Nineveh, respectively) rather than against Israel or Judah. They play a minor role in the overall prophetic picture. The postexilic prophets (Haggai, Zechariah, Malachi) likewise have a different message because they write after the Exile.

Jonah, however, is much more important to the basic prophetic message, even though he also preaches against a foreign city (Nineveh) and not against Israel or Judah. Our understanding of Jonah is that while the actual historical preached message is to the Ninevites, the literary message is an indictment against Israel and Judah. Jonah, one of the earliest prophets, sets up a foil for those that follow. The repentance of the foreign Ninevites stands in stark contrast to the obstinacy of the Israelites. What happens in Nineveh is what should be happening in Jerusalem and Samaria, but does not.

For example, Jeremiah preaches in Jerusalem for decades, and the response is only one of hostility. No one repents, from the greatest to the least of them. Jonah, by contrast, preaches a short, reluctant sermon in Nineveh (of all places!), and the entire city repents, from the greatest to the least. Jonah underscores how inexcusable the response of Israel and Judah is to the prophetic warning.

Conclusion

Whew! There is a lot of wonderful material in the Prophets. Certainly, these spokesmen from the Lord give us rich and deep teachings about the character of God. They also speak powerfully to us about our character and our behavior, using incredibly colorful and gripping poetic language that both sears and soars. Yet their basic message can be summarized into the three simple points as outlined above.

At the heart of their message, intertwined into all the different aspects of the prophetic word, we find the constant theme of God's relationship with his people. Studying the Prophets can help you to understand better the character of God and to grasp for yourself what God expects of you in your relationship with him and with your fellow human beings.

Discussion Questions

1. How does the fact that only a small percentage of Old Testament prophetic material deals with events that are still future to us influence our approach to interpreting prophecy?
2. In what specific ways do you think our culture needs to hear the message of the prophets?
3. What is your favorite passage from the Prophets? Why?

Writing Assignment

Apply the Interpretive Journey to either Micah 6:6–8 or Jeremiah 7:1–7. Answer the specific questions listed under Step 1 and then write a paragraph for each of the other steps.

> Step 1: Grasp the text in their town. What did the text mean to the biblical audience?

Study the text and make as many observations as you can. Mark the observations on a photocopy of the text (you can copy over the passage into a Word document from electronic sources, such as CD-ROM or the Internet, and add space between lines). Be sure you understand the meanings of all of the words. Do background study as needed to understand each term. Be sure to identify all figures of speech.

Identify the literary context and the historical-cultural context. When and where does this prophecy occur? (Use a Bible dictionary, handbook, or commentary to help you if need be.) What does the surrounding text discuss? Does this passage fall into one of the three main points of the prophetic message or one of the indictments discussed above? If so, which one? Review the discussion above regarding the point of the prophetic message that relates to your passage.

> Step 2: Measure the width of the river to cross. What are the differences between the biblical audience and us?
>
> Step 3: Cross the principlizing bridge. What is the theological principle in this text?
>
> Step 4: Cross into the New Testament. Does the New Testament teaching modify or qualify this principle, and, if so, how?
>
> Step 5: Grasp the text in our town. How should individual Christians today apply the theological principle in their lives?

15

O LORD, our Lord,
>   how majestic is your name in all the earth!

Some of the most beautiful and beloved passages in the Bible are found in the book of Psalms. Christians throughout the ages have turned to this book for encouragement in difficult times, and their spirits have been lifted and their hearts refreshed by the colorful and powerful poetry of the Psalter. Indeed, the psalms have a way of resonating within us — they reach down inside and vibrate within our souls, speaking to us quietly but powerfully. This phenomenon is universal. Regardless of age, education, or culture, Christians around the world cherish the psalms.

Reading the Psalms as Poetry

It is important to keep in mind that the psalms are written in Hebrew poetry and thus are quite different from New Testament books. Hebrew poetry is characterized by *terseness*, *a high degree of structure*, and *figurative imagery*.

Terseness simply means that poetry uses a minimum number of words. The words are chosen carefully for their impact and their power. Narrative texts frequently have long, descriptive sentences, but poetic texts are comprised of short, compact lines of verse with few words.

Structure refers primarily to the common feature of Old Testament poetry in which the text is structured around poetic lines of verse rather than around sentences and paragraphs. Punctuation is not nearly as important in poetry as it is in narrative or in New Testament letters. A line unit represents more of the thought unit than the sentence does. So train your eye to read line by line rather than sentence by sentence.

Furthermore, the lines are usually grouped in units of two or three. That is, two lines of Old Testament poetry are grouped together to express one thought. Most of the verses in the psalms are structured this way. For example, take a look at Psalm 3:1–2:

> O Lord, how many are my foes!
>> How many rise up against me!
> Many are saying of me,
>> "God will not deliver him."

This feature is called *parallelism*, and it is the dominant structural characteristic of Old Testament poetry. Usually one thought will be expressed by two lines of text (although occasionally the poets will use three or even four lines of text to convey one thought). Often the verse notations will follow this pattern, and each verse will consist of two lines of text. Such verse notations help us read because we need to interpret the text by reading each parallel construction together. That is, we look for two lines to convey one idea or thought.

Figurative imagery is the major medium through which the writers of the psalms communicate. They do not write essays; they paint pictures. The colors with which they paint these pictures are figures of speech and wordplays. We are not strangers to this type of language. English is rich in figurative language. We use figures of speech all the time.

In Psalms, practically every verse contains a figure of speech. Keep in mind that this does not in any way deny the literal reality behind the figure of speech. The authors are conveying real thoughts, events, and emotions to us—that is, *literal* truth—but they express this truth figuratively. Our job as readers is to grapple with the figures and to strive to grasp the reality and the emotion that the poets are conveying by their figurative language.

The Function of the Psalms

We agree with Fee and Stuart that the psalms "do not function primarily for the teaching of doctrine or moral behavior."[26] We caution you strongly against interpreting Psalms in the same fashion as you would Romans, which does focus on the teaching of doctrine and moral behavior. The psalms definitely have doctrinal components, and they also speak to moral behavior (Psalm 1), but those elements are corollaries or subpoints and not generally the intended focal point. Fee and Stuart write:

> The difficulty with interpreting the psalms arises primarily from their nature—what they are. Because the Bible is God's Word, many Christians automatically assume that all it contains are words *from* God *to* people. Thus they fail to recognize that the Bible also contains words spoken *to* God or *about* God—which is what the psalms do—and that these words, too, are God's Word.[27]

The function of the psalms, therefore, is to "give us inspired models of how to talk and sing to God."[28] In addition, the psalms provide us with inspired models of how to meditate about God—that is, how to think reflectively about God and what he has done for us. This interactive communication in Psalms between people and God can take place in numerous different contexts, reflecting the wide variety of life experiences from which people encounter God.

In general, the psalms can be categorized roughly into three main contexts of human life: (1) "seasons of well-being that evoke gratitude for the constancy of blessing," (2) "anguished seasons of hurt, alienation, suffering, and death," and (3) seasons of "surprise when we are overwhelmed with the new gifts of God, when joy breaks through the despair."[29]

Thus, even though Psalms is God's Word to us, it does not present specific doctrinal guidelines, but rather offers examples of how to communicate our deepest emotions and needs to God. When a psalmist cries out in anguish and despair, for example, the point or lesson is not that we also should cry out in despair. Rather, the lesson is that when we find ourselves in despair, it is right and proper for us, like the psalmist, to cry out in anguish and pain to God. As we do so, we can begin to experience his comfort and indeed be lifted "out of the slimy pit, out of the mud and mire" (Psalm 40:2).

Interpreting Psalms

Interpreting Psalms involves making the Interpretative Journey. You haven't forgotten the steps of the Journey, have you? Let's apply them to a representative Old Testament poetic text, Psalm 116:1–4.

Step 1: Grasp the text in their town. What did the text mean to the biblical audience? We begin with a close reading of the passage. Remember what you learned in chapters 2 and 3! Don't forget how to read carefully and make observations! As part of your close observation in Psalm 116:1–4, be sure to note the parallelism as discussed above. Combine the parallel passages into thoughts or images and then study the passage thought by thought. This will often involve reading two lines as one thought rather than reading one line at a time or one sentence at a time.

The opening verses of Psalm 116 can be divided into the following basic thoughts, based on parallelism:

Thought 1	I love the LORD, for he heard my voice; he heard my cry for mercy.
Thought 2	Because he turned his ear to me, I will call on him as long as I live.
Thought 3	The cords of death entangled me, the anguish of the grave came upon me; I was overcome by trouble and sorrow.
Thought 4	Then I called on the name of the LORD: "O LORD, save me!"

Next, *locate and visualize each figure of speech*. First, try to visualize the image. For example, explore the image in Thought 2 ("because he turned his ear to me"). People will often tilt their head or turn their head toward the source of a sound in order to hear well. Can you visualize the psalmist crying out to God, who, in response, turns his head to listen carefully? What about Thought 3? We see ropes coming up out of an open grave wrapping around the psalmist's legs and pulling him down into the grave.

Then be sure to *enter into the emotional world of the image.* Feel the comfort the psalmist has when he sees God turn his head to listen to him. Imagine the nightmare conveyed by the cords of death image! Ropes are wrapped around you and are pulling you down into a creepy, shadowy, open grave. You fall into the grave and scream for help! Death has a hold on you, but God hears your cry and reaches down to pull you out. This could come right out of a Stephen King movie!

Now we are ready to *summarize what the text meant for the biblical audience.* Keep in mind that these figures of speech were figures of speech for the ancient readers as well. Don't try to make the images literal for them but figurative for us. The writer of Psalm 116 was not being pulled down into a grave by cords literally. The message of Psalm 116:1–4 in their town is as follows: The writer is facing an immediate, scary, difficult situation. He may even be close to death itself. He calls out to God, who listens to him and then delivers him from the situation. Because of this, he expresses his love for God.

Step 2: Measure the width of the river to cross. What are the differences between the biblical audience and us? Of course, one of the central differences to remember always when crossing the river from the Old Testament is that we as New Testament believers are under a different covenant. While this is not a critical difference for the message of Psalm 116, it is always a factor to keep in mind. What other differences are there? We may not be in as frightening or difficult a situation as the psalmist was. (Yet some of us probably are.) We may not be facing imminent death.

Another important difference is that the Old Testament focuses on a different view of death than the New Testament does. There is little in the Old Testament about the afterlife (resurrection and heaven). The Old Testament doctrine on death is vague and shadowy. The assurance of eternal life is a doctrine that blossomed after Jesus' life, death, and resurrection.

Step 3: Cross the principlizing bridge. What is the theological principle in this text? A theological principle in Psalm 116:1–4 is that God's people should express their love to him when he hears them and delivers them from difficult and frightening situations such as death.

Step 4: Cross into the New Testament. Does the New Testament teaching modify or qualify this principle, and if so, how? The New Testament reaffirms the principle that we should express our love to God for having delivered us from difficult situations. In addition, the New Testament has much to say about our deliverance from death (and sin). First Corinthians 15 discusses this at length, explaining how God through Jesus has given us victory over death. We are promised resurrection and given eternal life. Those without Christ are staring death in the face and the "cords of the grave" do indeed pull them in. We also were in this predicament before we came to Christ, but God heard our cry and delivered us.

Note, however, that neither the New Testament nor the Old Testament teaches that God always intervenes to save us from all difficult, physical situations. God's people suffer and die physically throughout the Bible. Christians still get cancer and die. Car accidents still occur. For Christians, however, death never really wins. The cords never really get us in the grave. Christ has defeated the power of death, and he gives us victory over death.

Step 5: Grasp the text in our town. How should individual Christians apply this modified theological principle in their lives? Applications vary, depending on our situation. For Christians facing death, this text should give assurance that God will deliver us from the power of death through resurrection and eternal life, and we should express love to God for such deliverance. We should remember too the times when he delivered us from other difficult situations. And we should also express our love to God for saving us from eternal death.

Discussion Questions

1. Why should we not read Psalms in the same way that we read Romans?
2. How does understanding more about Hebrew poetry help us read the book of Psalms more responsibly?
3. Why is it important to observe the emotional dimension of the psalms?

Writing Assignment

Follow the directions below, completing all three parts of the assignment.

1. Read through Psalm 1 several times. Find and mark as many observations as you can on a photocopy of the text.
2. Describe and define the figures of speech in each verse.
3. Make the Interpretive Journey by completing the following:

Step 1: Grasp the text in their town. Give a one- or two sentencesummary of what the text meant to the biblical audience.

Step 2: Measure the width of the river to cross. What are the differences between the biblical audience and us? Identify the major differences.

Step 3: Cross the principlizing bridge. What is the theological principle in this text? Synthesize the passage into one basic principle.

Step 4: Cross into the New Testament. Does the New Testament teaching modify or qualify this principle, and if so, how?

Step 5: Grasp the text in our town. How should individual Christians apply this modified theological principle in their lives? Describe a specific way of applying this psalm in your own life.

Notes

1. This famous anecdote first appeared in 1940 in the *New York Times* as part of an advertisement for Mortimer J. Adler's work *How to Read a Book* (New York: Simon & Schuster, 1940). It is cited by Robert Traina, *Methodical Bible Study: A New Approach to Hermeneutics* (Kentucky: Asbury Theological Seminary, 1952), 97–98.

2. William Klein, Craig Blomberg, and Robert Hubbard, *Introduction to Biblical Interpretation*, 2nd ed. (Nashville: Word, 2003), 229.

3. Craig L. Blomberg, *1 Corinthians* (NIV Application Commentary; Grand Rapids: Zondervan, 1994), 228–29.

4. Craig Keener, *IVP Bible Background Commentary: New Testament* (Downers Grove, IL: InterVarsity, 1993), 60.

5. Robert H. Stein, *A Basic Guide to Interpreting the Bible: Playing by the Rules* (Grand Rapids: Baker, 1994), 75–76.

6. Kevin J. Vanhoozer, *Is There a Meaning in This Text? The Bible, the Reader, and the Morality of Literary Knowledge* (Grand Rapids: Zondervan, 1998), 346.

7. James W. Sire, *Scripture Twisting: 20 Ways the Cults Misread the Bible* (Downers Grove, IL: InterVarsity Press, 1980).

8. Klein, Blomberg, and Hubbard, *Biblical Interpretation*, 215.

9. For a discussion of English translations prior to 1611 and The Authorized Version of 1611 (King James Version), see J. Scott Duvall and J. Daniel Hays, *Grasping God's Word*, 2nd ed. (Grand Rapids: Zondervan, 2005), 160–64.

10. The *Textus Receptus* (Latin for "received text") was the Greek text published in the mid-1500s and used by the translators of the KJV. It was "received" in the sense that it was considered the standard Greek text of that time.

11. The following is a summary of only a few differences discussed by D. A. Carson in *The Inclusive-Language Debate* (Grand Rapids: Baker, 1998), 48–51.

12. Mark L. Strauss, *Distorting Scripture?* (Downers Grove, IL: InterVarsity Press, 1998), 77.

13. The following Wikipedia website describes in great detail the political interpretation of *The Wonderful Wizard of Oz*: http://en.wikipedia.org/wiki/ Political_interpretations_of_The_Wonderful_Wizard_of_Oz

14. This definition is based on that suggested by E. D. Hirsch, *Validity in Interpretation* (New Haven, CT: Yale Univ. Press, 1967), 8.

15. D. A. Carson and Douglas J. Moo, *An Introduction to the New Testament*, 2nd ed. (Grand Rapids: Zondervan, 2005), 331.

16. Gordon D. Fee and Douglas Stuart, *How to Read the Bible for All Its Worth*, 3rd ed. (Grand Rapids: Zondervan, 2003), 64.

17. Jack Kuhatschek, *Applying the Bible* (Grand Rapids: Zondervan, 1990), 57–61.

18. Sometimes determining what is cultural or time-bound in a text and what is normative or timeless presents a challenge. If you want to learn more about this issue, we recommend reading the discussion in Klein, Blomberg, and Hubbard, *Biblical Interpretation*, 487–98.

19. See Darrell L. Bock, "The Words of Jesus in the Gospels: Live, Jive, or Memorex?" in *Jesus Under Fire: Modern Scholarship Reinvents the Historical Jesus*, ed. Michael J. Wilkins and J. P. Moreland (Grand Rapids: Zondervan, 1995), 84–85.

20. See the more complete discussion in Duvall and Hays, *Grasping God's Word*, 256–61.

21. Cited in Fee and Stuart, *How to Read the Bible*, 150.

22. Craig Blomberg, *Interpreting the Parables* (Downers Grove, IL: InterVarsity Press, 1990).

23. For a fuller discussion of this issue, see Duvall and Hays, *Grasping God's Word*, 273–79.

24. For a fuller discussion of this issue, see Duvall and Hays, *Grasping God's Word*, 288–94.

25. Fee and Stuart, *How to Read the Bible*, 182.

26. Ibid., 205.

27. Ibid.

28. Robert B. Chisholm, *From Exegesis to Exposition* (Grand Rapids: Baker, 1998), 225.

29. Walter Brueggemann, *The Message of the Psalms* (Minneapolis: Augsburg, 1984), 19.

Index